LEARNING & TEACHING CENTRE
UNIVERSITY OF VICTORIA
PO BOX 1700 STN CSC
VICTORIA BC V8W 2Y2
CANADA

Assessing
Online
Learning

Assessing Online Learning

Patricia Comeaux

University of North Carolina–Wilmington

Editor

ANKER PUBLISHING COMPANY, INC.

Published by Jossey-Bass
A Wiley Imprint
989 Market Street, San Francisco, CA 94103-1741   www.josseybass.com

Library of Congress Cataloging-in-Publication Data

Comeaux, Patricia.
  Assessing online learning / Patricia Comeaux.
    p. cm.
  Includes bibliographical references and index.
  ISBN-13: 978-1882982-77-6
  ISBN-10: 1-882982-77-0
  1. Distance education—United States—Evaluation—Case studies. 2. Educational technology—United States—Evaluation—Case studies. 3. Community colleges—United States—Evaluation—Case studies. I. Title.
LB2328.15.U6C64 2005
371.35'8—dc22   2004013279

Printed in the United States of America
FIRST EDITION
HB Printing   10 9 8 7 6 5 4 3 2 1

Dedication

I dedicate this book and the writing process to my partner, colleague, best critic, and friend—Richard Huber—who loves to tinker with technological applications and, in doing so, opens up a world of possibilities for me, for other friends and colleagues, and for his students.

About the Authors

THE EDITOR

PATRICIA COMEAUX is a professor in the Department of Communication Studies at the University of North Carolina–Wilmington. Early in her university teaching career (1983), she discovered the value of an interdisciplinary approach to teaching and research when she designed and developed a communication-across-the-curriculum program at Illinois Wesleyan University. Since then, her teaching and research interests have been in observing and examining communication and learning in institutions of higher education. In the last 12 years, her research has focused on communication and learning in distance education settings. She has served as an outside project evaluator for a number of distance education–funded projects. In addition, she has published numerous articles on collaborative learning in higher education and the impact of interactive technologies on communication and learning. She recently edited a book on the topic titled *Communication and Collaboration in the Online Classroom: Examples and Applications* (Anker, 2002). She can be reached at comeauxp@uncw.edu.

THE CONTRIBUTORS

LIAM BANNON is a professor in the Department of Computer Science and Information Systems and director of the Interaction Design Centre at the University of Limerick, Ireland. His research and publications are in conceptual foundations of human-centered design, with a focus on collaborative practices, participatory design, and evaluation issues. He is a founding editor of the *CSCW Journal.* He is the co-editor of several books, including *Perspectives on the Computer Revolution* (Ablex, 1989). He can be reached at liam.bannon@ul.ie.

KAREN BELFER is a project manager/course developer of distance education and technology, and the coordinator of the ePortfolio Project at the University of British Columbia. Previously, she was the program evaluation and assessment coordinator of the Technical University of British Columbia where she designed and built a quality assurance structure for the development and delivery of online and mixed-mode courses. Her research interests include the assessment of online social learning environments, learning objectives, and teamwork. She can be reached at karen.belfer@ubc.ca.

BRUCE BURNETT is a lecturer in the School of Cultural and Language Studies in Education at Queensland University of Technology, Australia. He has a primary disciplinary background in sociology and in particular the sociocultural links between students and technology. He is currently lecturing on new technologies and new literacies and has published internationally on the pedagogical aspects of higher education's move into the online environment. He can be reached at b.burnett@qut.edu.au.

ELE MCKENNA-BYINGTON is an associate professor in the Department of English at the University of North Carolina–Wilmington (UNCW). She is a former director of the composition program at UNCW and co-editor of a textbook for college writing and reading courses, *Critical Issues in Contemporary Cultures* (Longman, 1997). She has received several development grants to design and teach two online writing courses and an online linguistics course. She has also published the results of teaching online in Patricia Comeaux's edited collection, *Communication and Collaboration in the Online Classroom: Examples and Applications* (Anker, 2002). She can be reached at byingtone@uncw.edu.

TONY HALL is a research officer in the Interaction Design Centre at the University of Limerick, Ireland. He is currently working on the European Union Disappearing Computer Project, SHAPE, exploring the use of novel computer technologies to enhance the educational and social function of museums. He worked previously as an instructional designer, secondary teacher, and web designer. His research interests and publications encompass the design, implementation, and evaluation of technologies to enhance learning and pedagogy. He is a member of a number of associations and societies for research in learning and instruction. He can be reached at tony.hall@ul.ie.

DAVID HOFMEISTER is a professor and chair of Curriculum, Instruction, and Media Technology at Indiana State University. In the late 1990s he initiated Virtual Literature Circles, a project that links elementary students together through message boards to discuss literature. From that initial project, several additional discussion-based learning projects emerged. His research interests focus on community building and cognitive complexity measures in the use of message boards and various communication devices. He can be reached at eshofmei@isugw.indstate.edu.

CONOR MOLAN is a graduate student in business administration at the University of Limerick, Ireland, where he graduated in 2003 with a B.Sc. in computer systems. Previously, he worked with Fidelity Investments Systems Company as a quality assurance engineer. His academic interests include business information systems, the deployment of e-marketing, and management technology. He can be reached at conormolan@hotmail.com.

EAMONN MURPHY is Boart Longyear Professor of Quality and Applied Statistics at the University of Limerick, Ireland. He is widely published in the statistics and quality management fields. His recent research interests are in e-learning, particularly the use of new technologies to enhance the teaching of mathematics and statistics in third-level and university education. He is also research director of the Centres for Quality Management and Advanced Manufacturing Technology at the University of Limerick. He can be reached at eamonn.murphy@ul.ie.

MAHNAZ MOALLEM is an associate professor of instructional technology and program coordinator (and an original designer) of the Master's Program in Instructional Technology at the University of North Carolina–Wilmington. She teaches courses in instructional systems design, instructional technology, and classroom assessment and evaluation. Her main area of scholarship is instructional design theories, models, and principles. She has authored many articles in her field and is currently writing a book, *Instructional Design for Teachers*. Her articles are published in journals such as *Instructional Technology Research and Development* and *Educational Foundations*. She can be reached at moallemm.@uncw.edu.

BOLANLE A. OLANIRAN is a professor in the Department of Communication Studies at Texas Tech University. His research interests and publications are in the area of computer-mediated communication, specifically exploring the role and effects of communication technologies in organizations and student learning. He has received recognition and consulting opportunities from both private and government agencies, including the assessment of video conferencing at the Department of Commerce–U.S. Census Bureau (2001). He can be reached at B.Olaniran@ttu.edu.

MARINA ORSINI-JONES is a senior lecturer and coordinator of the Centre for Information Technology in Language Learning at Coventry University, England. She currently teaches Italian language and society, professional and academic skills, and teaching and learning theory and practice. She has published work on the evaluation of online learning based upon the use of WebCT at Coventry University in UK-based journals and international journals. She can be reached at m.orsini@coventry.ac.uk.

MARGOT PEREZ-GREENE is director of the National Institute for Staff and Organizational Development and lecturer in the Community College Leadership Program in the Department of Educational Administration at the University of Texas–Austin. Prior to coming to the University of Texas in August 1999, she served as vice president of enrollment management and student development at Iowa Central Community College. She can be reached at mpg@mail.utexas.edu.

ALAN ROBERTS is a lecturer in the School of Cultural and Language Studies in Education at Queensland University of Technology, Australia. His primary discipline is in the area of technology education. He is currently lecturing and consulting in the use of technology in team development and in the use of constructivist learning paradigms to design online instruction. His research interests focus on optimizing engagement and knowledge-building within computer-supported collaborative environments. He can be reached at ag.roberts@qut.edu.au.

MARIANNA SIGALA is a lecturer in operations and production management in the Department of Business Administration at the University of the Aegean, Greece. She teaches courses in business process, and information and communication technologies (ICT). Her major research interests and publications are in ICT applications management and in hospitality and tourism operations and education, specifically in the development and evaluation of e-learning pedagogy and models. Her work has been published in several international journals and conferences. She can be reached at m.sigala@aegean.gr.

MATT THOMAS is an associate professor of literacy education in the Department of Curriculum and Instruction at Central Missouri State University where he teaches courses on content area literacy. His publication record and research agenda focus on the integration of educational technology with traditional pedagogy, especially the use of online discussion boards in content area reading, writing, thinking, and interacting. He is the associate editor of the *Journal of Content Area Reading* and co-author of the fourth edition of *Content Area Literacy: Interactive Teaching for Active Learning* (Jossey-Bass, 2004). He can be reached at mthomas@cmsu1.cmsu.edu.

RON WAKKARY is an associate professor in information technology and interactive arts at Simon Fraser University, British Columbia. Previously, he was faculty in interactive arts and the dean of academic planning at the Technical University of British Columbia. His research interests include interaction design, collaborative authorship, and design theory. His writings have bridged many areas with design, including education. He can be reached at rwakkary@sfu.ca.

Contents

Foreword

My involvement with online assessment began while I was working on my second doctoral degree at a distance education institution. While my online learning experiences were quite positive, I was frustrated with the inconsistency in assessment practices. The quality of instructor feedback for my term papers and online discussion comments varied noticeably among classes. That experience prompted me to conduct a research project on interactivity (communication, participation, and feedback) in graduate distance education institutions.

My research results affirmed that students consider instructor assessment procedures as a relational prompt that transcends receiving grades on assignments. The absence of consistent feedback creates doubt in students' minds about their academic abilities and contributes to a more impersonal instructional experience. As I became more involved in distance education, I began to realize how the process of online assessment has a unique complexity that humbles the best of teachers!

I have enjoyed working online as a graduate instructor and mentor of faculty candidates for the University of Phoenix Online (UOP). My teaching strategies became more focused on assessment issues as I spent more time creating new grading practices to match the online academic setting. Contemporary distance education schools tend to stress more written assignments, and teachers use fewer tests and quizzes. Alternative assessments have become more popular with faculty members who feel they offer distinct advantages over more conventional assessment methods. Students are given a diversity of learning opportunities to display higher-order thinking skills and greater depth of knowledge, connect learning to their daily lives, and develop a deeper dialog over the course material.

After teaching numerous online classes, I am convinced that a key ingredient in assessment is communication. In fact, effective communication between teacher and students is essential to sophisticated learning experiences and a vital factor that helps learners successfully negotiate online classes. The student-centered model of learning encourages teachers to view their students as academic partners who work together to produce relevant and meaningful learning experiences. Assessment procedures need to foster a meaningful bridge between academic knowledge, skills, and experiences of the classroom to students' daily lives.

Patricia Comeaux has skillfully addressed vital assessment issues in *Assessing Online Learning.* It is an excellent resource for educators, administrators, and instructional course designers who desire expertise and practical advice on assessment teaching practices. The contributing authors, from a variety of disciplines, provide a wealth of strategies and tools for assessing online instruction and learning. It will make a significant contribution to assessment literature and encourage creative improvements in the teaching and learning process.

Brent Muirhead
Area Chair, MAED Curriculum and Technology
University of Phoenix Online
Associate Editor, *Educational Technology & Society*
Editor of Online Learning, *Journal of the United States Distance Learning Association*

Preface

The educational community in higher education has, for some time, debated assessment issues. However, with the proliferation of online classrooms and the emphasis on constructivist approaches to learning, issues of assessment have taken on even more importance than ever before. Although there are an increasing number of collections and texts about online teaching and learning, very little has been written about the particular needs and challenges of assessment in online instruction.

The question explored throughout this book is "How do we assess online learning?" The contributing authors make clear their underlying assumptions about assessment and learning as they describe and analyze their experiences with evaluating online programs and courses and their assessment practices in online classrooms. Thus, this book is both conceptual and pragmatic as it addresses the salient issues of assessment and offers a variety of assessment tools and strategies for online classrooms and programs.

This collection is written for faculty in higher education and offers an assortment of tools and strategies for evaluating learning as well as instructional design in online classrooms. It provides self-assessment tools for students to evaluate their progress toward their final products. It also provides instruments in which teams can evaluate their progress and contributions. Furthermore, it offers specific tools and strategies for assessing students' critical thinking and writing skills in electronic discussion boards and in similar reflective writing environments.

The uniqueness of this treatise is the focus on assessment as an integral part of learning. This collection builds on the paradigms of constructivist learning established in *Communication and Collaboration in the Online Classroom: Examples and Application* (Anker, 2002). Constructivist learning paradigms are learner centered and assert that learning occurs when students are actively engaged in making sense of phenomena as well as constructing and negotiating meanings with others.

In constructivist learning environments, assessment and learning are integrally linked. Consequently, effective communication becomes a key ingredient in assessment practices, especially in online environments. While the same is true of the relationships between effective communication assessment and learning in face-to-face classrooms, the demands of assessment are even more challenging in online environments. Without consistent, timely, and relevant feedback, online students more easily interpret their classroom experience as impersonal and a hindrance to their learning.

Because of the multidisciplinary and comprehensive approach to this book, it will be of interest to faculty, administrators, scholars, and researchers in higher education. Readers who have a particular interest in the topic of assessment and online learning will find this collection to be a valuable resource. The contributing authors, from a variety of disciplines, are nationally and internationally prominent educators who advocate and practice a constructivist approach to learning. They are experienced instructors in both face-to-face and online classrooms and they view assessment and learning as central components in their instructional design.

OVERVIEW OF CONTENTS

- *Introduction:* Patricia Comeaux reviews the relevant literature on learning and assessment and establishes the integral relationship between them. She also provides a content analysis of the book's chapters to serve as a guide for locating valuable strategies and tools throughout the book.

- *Chapter 1:* Margot Perez-Greene addresses the technology transformations affecting community colleges and the subsequent challenges that assessment and accountability have demanded. She describes how eight community colleges in the United States have addressed those assessment challenges.

- *Chapter 2:* Mahnaz Moallem illustrates how to use collaborative learning techniques to challenge graduate students and enhance the true acquisition of knowledge. She provides examples of how to evaluate products and performances designed with specific goals and standards of success. She details how to measure and monitor these projects using student self-assessment and expert assessment checklists and rubrics.

- *Chapter 3:* Karen Belfer and Ron Wakkary provide guidelines and checklists for team assessment for an undergraduate course in interaction design. They also offer guidelines in team assessment that account for individual contributions as well as group activity.

- *Chapter 4:* Bruce Burnett and Alan Roberts describe assessment models developed in two Australian university undergraduate bachelor of education units. Both models make extensive use of employing technology as a tool to think with. They provide strategies and assessment methods for using these models to guide students' learning as they work together on authentic tasks (which can be used in their future careers).

- *Chapter 5:* David Hofmeister and Matt Thomas present a detailed description of Virtual Learning Modules (VLM), which are elaborately organized readings and questions located on electronic discussion boards. They provide rubrics for assessing students' writings through a VLM and suggestions for structuring and moderating online discussions with questions that challenge students to think and write more analytically.

- *Chapter 6:* Marianna Sigala describes and analyzes a model for examining the relationship between online performance and the quality of participation by students in online forums. The evaluation tool for assessment is based on a model for analyzing the content of discussion transcripts. She applies this model to an online debate and provides suggestions and tools for developing successful online learning assignments and assessment.

- *Chapter 7:* Tony Hall, Conor Molan, Liam Bannon, and Eamonn Murphy describe the redesign of the online component of a blended learning course developed to enhance the teaching of statistics to third-level engineering, mathematics, and computer science students. They describe the development and uses of interactive digital video to help students understand *why* their answers on an online multiple-choice test are right or wrong. They argue that the video-augmented multiple-choice questions increased students' understanding and application of the course concepts.

- *Chapter 8:* Ele Byington describes the development, teaching, and assessment processes involved in teaching an online course in linguistics. She describes how online multiple choice tests and true/false tests can provide advantages not available in face-to-face classrooms. She also describes her online assessment practices for an essay-writing course and compares the assessment practices for both courses.

- *Chapter 9:* Marina Orsini-Jones describes how a team of linguists worked in partnership with a library staff to develop online assessments of students' subject-specific library skills. She provides examples of online multiple-choice questions and timed essays which assessed students' online navigation and information retrieval skills.

- *Chapter 10:* Bolanle A. Olaniran presents an analysis and evaluation of a course combining both face-to-face (FtF) interaction and computer-mediated communication (CMC). He provides suggestions on how to evaluate the benefits and challenges of a combined CMC/FtF course, as well as its effects on student learning and technological acceptance.

Patricia Comeaux
March 2004

Introduction

Assessment and Learning

Patricia Comeaux

Suddenly I saw things differently, and
because I saw differently, I thought differently,
I felt differently, and I behaved differently.
—Covey, 1989, p. 31

How do we, in higher education, view assessment, and how does it fit into our educational practices? Is it something we consider after instructional design or do we view assessment as an integral part of instruction and learning? With increased emphasis on accountability in general (e.g., American Association for Higher Education's 2002 assessment conference) and increased scrutiny of online teaching and learning, issues of assessment have taken on more importance than ever before.

The question explored in this introductory chapter and throughout the book is "How do we assess online learning?" The contributing authors make clear their underlying assumptions about assessment and learning as they describe and analyze their experiences with evaluating online programs and courses and their assessment practices in online classrooms. Thus, this book is both conceptual and pragmatic as it addresses the salient issues of assessment, and it offers a variety of assessment tools and strategies for online classrooms and programs.

Any treatise on assessment must first establish the underlying paradigm of learning on which it is based. Therefore, I review the relevant literature on learning and assessment, establishing the integral relationship between them. In addition, I provide a content analysis of the chapters in this collection, which serves as a guide for locating valuable strategies and tools throughout the book.

LEARNER-CENTERED PARADIGMS AND ASSESSMENT

Scholars and researchers from a variety of disciplines (communication, education, instructional technology, and distance education) argue that learning is a complex, collaborative process based on constructivist philosophies and active learning methodologies (for an extensive review and analysis of this literature, see Comeaux, 2002). Constructivist learning paradigms are learner centered and posit that learning occurs when students are actively engaged in making sense of phenomena as well as constructing and negotiating meanings with others. They emphasize the interdependence of the learners and the communal nature of the process as knowledge that is negotiated and constructed through dialogue, problem solving, and authentic experiences. Such paradigms further assume that instructors and students reverse roles in the reciprocal processes of teaching and learning. Thus, learning is a reflective and analytical practice as well as an intellectual transformative act. It works when it engages students in active, co-responsible ways of knowing so that teaching and learning become reciprocal enterprises as teachers and learners coexist in a communal space of shaping and transforming knowledge and understanding.

Furthermore, scholars and researchers who acknowledge that learning is a complex collaborative process view assessment as an integral part of learning (Anderson, 1998; Angelo & Cross, 1993; Boud, 1995a; Huba & Freed, 2000; Reeves & Okey, 1996; Sanders, 2001; Speck, 2002). This view of assessment recognizes that knowledge has multiple meanings and that learning is an active, collaborative process. It emphasizes the importance of assessing process (formative) as well as product (summative). As Speck (2002) explains, ". . . professors in such classrooms will design assignments that allow for interplay between process and product, between formative and summative assessment" (p. 15).

Furthermore, this paradigm of assessment claims that an important function of assessment is to facilitate and promote learning. As Huba and Freed (2000) explain,

> We can both encourage and shape the type of learning we desire through the types of assessment we use. . . . Assessment is the process of gathering and discussing informa-

tion from multiple and diverse sources in order to develop a deep understanding of what students know, understand, and can do with their knowledge as a result of their educational experiences; the process culminates when assessment results are used to improve subsequent learning. (p. 8)

In learner-centered environments, instructors provide students with the characteristics or standards of excellence to which practicing professionals in their disciplines are held. In these learning environments, assignments or projects are analogous to the kinds of real-world problems faced by citizens, consumers, or professionals in the field. Thus, assignments emerge from authentic tasks and engage learners in meaningful, problem-based thinking and reflection.

Learner-centered assessment "will drive and shape learning outcomes ... [and] encourage purposeful dialogue, multiple discourses, collaboration, peer and self-evaluation, and contribute to a sense of community and shared purpose [among learners and instructor]" (Morgan & O'Reilly, 2001, p. 185). In these learning environments, students are aware from the onset what is expected of them; they know they are expected to demonstrate understanding of the subject matter and apply their understanding in authentic situations. Romer and the Education Commission of the States (1996) reports that "Students learn more effectively when expectations for learning are placed at high but attainable levels, and when these expectations are communicated clearly from the onset" (p. 5). Boud (1995b) makes a similar claim when he explains that our assessment methods and requirements probably have a greater influence on how and what learners learn than any other single factor.

Because assessment events drive learning outcomes, as the literature reveals, they are integral to the design and structure of not only a particular subject but also the learning environment. As educators and scholars, we *must* critically assess the characteristics and quality of online learning environments, and we must also consider how technology impacts assessment. Interactive technologies provide us with a vast collection of resources that can enhance and extend learning environments and open up a world of possibilities in instructional design and assessment. The contributing authors in this collection represent a variety of disciplines and provide a wealth of assessment tools and strategies that enable online instructors and learners to evaluate their experiences and to consider the power of interactive technologies.

PREVIEW AND CONTENT ANALYSIS OF THE CHAPTERS

The book's contributors support and extend a learner-centered view of assessment. They recognize learning as an active, collaborative process occurring in environments in which instructors and students engage in co-responsible activities for assessing learning. They provide specific assessment tools and strategies for assessing online learning and describe the potential in using technology to support assessment. They also describe several functions of technology that illustrate its ability to enhance and improve both learning and assessment of learning.

Chapters requirements for this book specified that they should be pragmatic and provide assessment tools and strategies as well as ways to use them in online classrooms. I was pleased to rediscover these specifications as I conducted a content analysis of the selected chapters. The following sections represent the result of a content analysis of the 10 chapters selected for this collection. My analysis revealed six themes that are prevalent in this book.

- Interactive technologies provide multiple benefits in assessing learning.

- Authentic tasks (assignments) enhance the learning environment and make assessment more meaningful.

- Assessment rubrics and instruments provide learners with clear expectations for accomplishing their assigned tasks.

- Structuring guided questions and providing clear criteria for assessing contributions in electronic discussion boards foster critical thinking and analysis.

- Multiple-choice tests can enhance constructive learning environments.

- Assessment practices are valuable for improving learning, instruction, and program development.

While the table of contents provides a generic overall guide to the chapters, the themes and tables below provide a more specific guide to locating the book's valuable resources and information that can shape and guide online learning and assessment.

Benefits of Online Assessment

As the chapter authors describe, interactive technologies provide multiple advantages and benefits for online instructors and learners, including:

- More efficient management, collection, and transfer of assessment information

- The ability to track, monitor, and document students' activities automatically

- Multiple communication tools to facilitate and document dialogues that can be revisited as part of the learning process

- Unlimited and self-paced access to course materials

- More opportunities and ways for providing feedback to students

- Vast libraries of resources and interpretive tools

- Increased student participation in discussions (i.e., more students can participate in online asynchronous threaded discussions than in face-to-face classrooms)

- An increased emphasis on student thoughts and reflections as students learn to express their ideas in writing

- Allowing students to feel that they share a more democratic setting with their instructors, who become their peers in discussion forums

- Online tests free from the restrictions of time and place imposed on testing in face-to-face classrooms

Authentic Task Assignments and Assessment in Online Learning

Constructivist and learner-centered environments are enhanced when students are required to complete authentic tasks analogous to the kinds of products and performances required of practicing professionals. Throughout this book, there are a number of excellent examples of such authentic tasks created specifically for online learning environments. Table 1 provides the chapter location and the discipline for each authentic task listed.

Table 1
Chapter Location and Discipline for Authentic Tasks

Discipline/Course and Level	Authentic Task/Assignment and Chapter Location
Mathematics and Statistics, undergraduate level	Develop a narrative for a video in a statistical problem-solving situation (Chapter 7)
Instructional Technology, graduate level	Design and develop an instructional module for a professional context (Chapter 2)
Business Education, undergraduate level, pre-service	Develop a concept map and model to use in unit and lesson plan designs (Chapter 4)
Teacher Education/Language and Technology, undergraduate level	In teams, develop a web site report of selected topics based on individual's research (Chapter 4)
Instructional Design and Interactive Arts, undergraduate level	In teams, create an artistic product (video, performance, web site, etc.) (Chapter 3)

Constructing Rubrics and Assessment Tools for Online Environments

Throughout this collection, the contributing authors provide a useful assortment of rubrics and assessment tools for online environments. Table 2 provides a list of these instruments and their locations.

Table 2

Location of Assessment Instruments for Online Learning

How to construct a rubric—a scoring guide for assessment (Chapter 5)
Criteria checklist for constructing assessment tools for individuals and teams (Chapter 3)
Criteria for functionality of web site (Chapter 4)
Online questionnaire assessing instruction, course design, and web site (Chapter 7)
Criteria for assessing individual and team contributions (Chapter 3)
Self-assessment instrument for course assignment (Chapter 2)
Team assessment rubric for participation and contribution (Chapter 2)

Assessing Contributions in Electronic Discussion Boards

While electronic discussion boards have the potential to be excellent learning tools, they can be tedious and cumbersome without structure and guidance from instructors or moderators. Several of the book's authors address that potential problem by describing how to create questions that will help focus online discussions. In addition, they provide specific guidelines and criteria for assessing contributions in electronic discussion boards to foster critical thinking and analysis. Table 3 provides the location of these guidelines and criteria.

Table 3

Location of Tools for Assessing Contributions in Online Discussion Boards

Strategies for preparing and structuring questions to foster reflection and analysis (Chapter 5)
Instrument for assessing and scoring the level of reading, writing, and thinking skills in online discussion boards (Chapter 5)
Questions used in an online forum to guide and evaluate an education unit (Chapter 4)
Strategies and tools for structuring and assessing an online debate (Chapter 6)

Creating and Using Online Multiple-Choice Tests

Too often multiple-choice exams focus on recall and memorization. Consequently, instructors are understandably leery of using them in online environments. Several chapters in this book describe how multiple-choice tests can be used to further students' understanding of the topic and to develop critical thinking skills. Table 4 indicates which chapters provide examples of online multiple-choice tests and their values.

Table 4

Location of Strategies for Creating and Using Online Multiple-Choice Tests

WebCT features for creating online multiple-choice and true/false tests for online lecture-based courses (Chapter 8)
Strategies for creating and using online multiple-choice tests for assessing students' library skills in online navigation and information retrieval (Chapter 9)
Using online multiple-choice tests to help students understand mathematics and statistics (Chapter 7)

Assessment as a Way to Improve Instruction and Learning

One of the most valuable consequences of assessment tools and strategies is that they can be used to improve instructional design, student learning, and educational programs. There are several examples of these valuable uses of assessment throughout this collection. Table 5 indicates which chapters provide detailed descriptions of how online assessments were used for educational improvement.

Table 5

Location of Assessment Practices Used to Improve Instruction

Assessment practices used by representative community colleges in the United States (Chapter 1)
Strategies for using online assessment tools to improve a course and curriculum for a library skills unit in language usage for academic and professional contexts (Chapter 9)
Use of online assessment instruments and narrative video to assess student learning and improve instructional design for a mathematics and statistics course (Chapter 7)
Assessment instruments to guide and ensure the quality of the instructional design for team assignments and team participation for an interactive arts course (Chapter 3)
Use of online assessment of student learning to improve instructional design in teacher education courses (Chapter 4)
Strategies for evaluating a course (interpersonal communication) that used a combination of online discussion and face-to-face instruction (Chapter 10)

CLOSING

The uniqueness of this collection is its focus on assessment as an integral part of learning. As such, effective communication becomes a key ingredient in online assessment practices. While the same is true of the relationships among effective communication, assessment, and learning in the face-to-face classroom, the demands of assessment are even more challenging in online environments. Without consistent, timely, and relevant feedback, online students more easily interpret their classroom experience as impersonal and a hindrance to their learning.

This book illustrates the power of interactive technologies (computer-mediated communication) to enable conversation and collaboration among diverse communities of learners, thus enhancing and supporting constructivist learning environments.

1

Assessment Is on the Line in Community Colleges

Margot Perez-Greene

*The best thing for being sad, replied Merlyn . . . is to learn
something. That is the only thing that never fails. You may
grow old and trembling in your anatomies, you may lie
awake at night listening to the disorder of your veins, you
may see the world around you devastated by evil lunatics, or
know your honor trampled in the sewers of baser minds.
There is only one thing for it then—to learn. Learn why the
world wags and what wags it. That is the only thing which
the mind can never exhaust, never alienate, never be tor-
tured by, never fear or distrust, and never dream of regret-
ting. Learning is the thing for you.*
—T. H. White (as qtd. in Palmer, 1998, p. 141)

TECHNOLOGY IN COMMUNITY COLLEGES

One hundred and twelve institutions of higher education participated in
the Pew Higher Education Roundtable Program and were asked to identify the issues most prevalent on their campuses. Of the nine issues repeatedly noted by campus leaders, technology was the one most frequently
mentioned. Eighty-four percent of campus leaders indicated that more
effective use of technology in teaching and learning was the most important issue on their campuses, especially so among the 21 community colleges in the study (as cited in O'Banion, 1997, p. 65).

1

Community colleges cannot ignore technology and the impact it has on the business they conduct—advancing learning. Community college administrators and faculty have stepped up to the plate to address the effect that technology has in changing the practices and behaviors of instructional delivery, at a pace difficult to match.

Bill Gates writes about lessons he learned as chief executive officer for Microsoft in his first book, *The Road Ahead*. He offers the following points that emphasize the importance of maintaining a competitive edge, no matter what our business, because of the strong technology influence.

- We need to be technologically compatible with others.

- We need to compete and cooperate at the same time.

- We need to attract smart, energetic, entrepreneurial people, because smart people like to work with smart people.

- We need to be bold. We need to be wary of our successes. No product stays on top unless it is improved.

- We need a "killer application"—a use of technology so attractive to consumers that it fuels market forces and it makes an invention all but indispensable.

- We need to stick with our mission and continue using new technologies.

(as cited in O'Banion, 1997, pp. 70–73)

In his 1993 review of roughly three decades of instructional uses of computers in community colleges, the vice chancellor of education and technology at Metropolitan Community College argued that educators know much about technology and its use in transforming the teaching and learning process, noting an emphasis on the assessment of student learning and not on course materials (as cited in O'Banion, 1997, pp. 67–68). The focus is not on content but on the transferable skills that are the learning outcomes of courses and programs—the ability to gain access to information, interpret it, give it context, use information to solve problems, and collaborate with others in solving problems (as cited in O'Banion, 1997, pp. 67–68).

No doubt, technology has extended exceptionally good avenues for community colleges to provide distance-learning opportunities to students who are unwilling or unable to choose the traditional classroom setting, for a host of reasons. Community colleges have been identified as a critical link to creating a high-quality workforce that is required to maintain competition, the burden becoming significantly greater in light of the Workforce Investment Act of 1998.

TECHNOLOGY CALLS FOR COLLEGE-WIDE TRANSFORMATION

Technology completely affected education as we knew it in community colleges, and it has dramatically altered what is possible in teaching and learning. Huge challenges prevent immediate solutions to the technology drama staged on community college campuses across America. Community colleges face many technology battles.

- The high cost of technology and the all-too-familiar tight budget formulas regulated by individual states (familiar funding regulations), the most recent economic hardship brought on by the tragic events on September 11, 2001, and subsequent Iraq war

- Dynamic, rapidly advancing hardware and software products derail attempts to stay on course

- Serious workforce training programs that were desperately needed yesterday

- The need for professional development so that community college instructors, administrators, and staff can function successfully in their roles

- Technology-savvy students who have high expectations and shop the education marketplace intelligently

- Competitive "no-boundaries" markets for education that require flexibility in scheduling

- The acceptance of new technology principles and methods by the college community

- Disconnected, piecemeal infrastructures acquired over time that cause delay in providing services to everyone

Technology Plans

Colleges initially began developing campus-wide strategic technology plans in the 1980s and well into the 1990s that included comprehensive, well-documented strategies for implementation, which were considered long-range planning documents—five-, seven-, and even ten-year implementation schedules. As colleges experienced constant emerging trends and technological advancement at an unbelievable rate of change, these plans became outdated well before their time.

Most colleges undergo an annual revisiting of existing technology plans that, in many cases, include the input of the entire college community. Colleges also understand the need for ongoing assessment of student learning, instruction, and administrative services so that the essentials for all players involved comprise the plan. Colleges develop master plans that are very comprehensive and contain forecasts; intermediate, shorter-range planning; annual goals and objectives; hardware replacement and recycling guidelines; activity plans that change frequently; and yearly fiscal purchasing procedures.

Community colleges have also learned that plans must incorporate the most advanced technologies money can buy because today's college students have spent their lives surrounded by technology and expect colleges to be technologically adept. They are customers and, therefore, search for the best instructional environment so that they may advance educationally and leave with skills that will best prepare them for today's job market.

Assessment Is Vital to the Planning Process

The definition of assessment created by the Assessment Forum of the American Association for Higher Education reflects the goals and principles of the learning college and can be applied to the principles, policies, and procedures adopted by any institution of higher education as plans develop for online assessment.

> Assessment is an ongoing process aimed at understanding and improving student learning. It involves making our expectations explicit and public; setting appropriate criteria and high standards for learning quality; systematically gathering, analyzing, and interpreting evidence to determine how well performance matches those expectations and standards; and using the resulting information to document, explain, and improve performance. When it is embedded effectively within larger institutional systems, assessment can help us focus our collective attention, examine our assumptions, and create a shared academic

culture dedicated to assuring and improving the quality of higher education. (Angelo, 1995, p. 7)

Dissatisfaction with the state of education led to a meeting in Racine, Wisconsin, with leading educators whose task it was to review the literature on learning and provide a set of guiding principles that could assist in effecting learning. The outcome of this meeting was the creation of the Seven Principles for Good Practice in Undergraduate Education.

Good practice in undergraduate education:

1) Encourages contacts between students and faculty.

2) Develops reciprocity and cooperation among students.

3) Uses active learning techniques.

4) Gives prompt feedback.

5) Emphasizes time on task.

6) Communicates high expectations.

7) Respects diverse talents and ways of learning.
(Chickering & Gamson, 1987, p. 3)

Community colleges across America have convened teams to design assessment and planning processes for their colleges. These assessments analyze existing internal technological infrastructure to evaluate technology conditions by appraising their connectivity ability, technical support systems, professional development, and workforce needs. In addition, these judgments provide rigorous means for evaluating programs and assessing student learning. Much foundational work occurs before technology plans can be adopted for integration and implementation, and assessment of student learning must be included in the overall plan. Without it, the plan is useless.

THE PUBLIC COMMANDS ACCOUNTABILITY FROM INSTITUTIONS OF HIGHER LEARNING

It is not sufficient to rest on the laurels of past success or the record of the present. For all its rich history, there are too many signs that higher education is not taking seriously its responsibility to maintain a strong commitment to undergraduate learning; to be accountable for products that are relevant, effective, and of demonstrable quality; and to provide society with the full benefits from investments in research and public service. Thus, the challenge to higher education is to be sufficiently responsive and adaptable in light of these new demands and to propel our nation to the forefront of a new era. Unless political leaders, educators, and the public accept this challenge, higher education soon may be a worn-out system that has seen its best days. (as qtd. in Roueche, Johnson, Roueche, & Associates, 1997, p. 25)

Assessment becomes increasingly difficult as colleges offer more online courses for the "anywhere, anytime" learner. Nonetheless, public demand for accountability in all aspects of higher education has increased tremendously, especially in the area of resource stewardship and, most recently, student learning. For this reason, colleges are mobilized to provide evidence of learning by taking rigorous steps to revamp plans that more clearly define goals, objectives, and evaluation practices that lead to assessing the outcome they desire for their students—learning!

Peggy Maki (2001), director of assessment for the American Association for Higher Education, states that assessment generally seeks to answer the following questions:

- What are we trying to do and why?

- What is my program supposed to accomplish?

- How well are we doing?

- How do we know how well we are doing?

- How do we use the information to improve or celebrate successes?

- Do the improvements we make work?

Community colleges are taking giant leaps to ensure that learning is occurring within their newfound structures of online course delivery. Assessment techniques and procedures are experimental, infantile, and a struggle, at best. Many find assessment of online courses extremely time-consuming and, unquestionably, not yet fully researched. However, visionary community colleges labor to stay focused on the outcomes of their learners while maintaining quality in the traditional classroom and measuring their impact in both venues.

COMMUNITY COLLEGES WORK FERVENTLY TO MEASURE STUDENT LEARNING

The infusion of technology adds new dimensions to the learning process. Faculty may wish to reacquaint themselves with the framework developed by Cleveland (as cited in O'Banion, 1997, pp. 99–100) that serves to distinguish old learning from new learning principles (see Table 1.1). This table is included as a reference to promulgate the complexity of the human brain and to draw attention to the alignment between new learning principles and the experiences online learning presents.

Twigg (2002) adds encouragement by explaining that online courses carry with them continuous assessment and are viewed by students as learning experiences as opposed to all-or-nothing performance measures. She further adds that students in online courses are spending more time studying, gaining a higher level of familiarity with tested material and comfort with the testing process, and receiving immediate feedback that provides regular information about their progress and achievement. Furthermore, making corrections in a timely manner provides students with a greater understanding of the content. And, threading assessment continuously throughout a course can enhance learning.

Community colleges are fortunate to have an assortment of commercially available assessment options in addition to adapted, traditionally used tools, techniques, methods, and processes to assess student learning. The choice of the assessment tool applied is largely dependent on the course, the level of student ability, and the level of instructor technical skill and knowledge. A number of them are offered below.

- Final projects that demonstrate knowledge and skill level

- Journals well suited to reflect change over time

- Commercial management tools that embody their own strategies, techniques, and processes

- Printed or online tests

Table 1.1

New Views of Learning

Old Learning	New Learning
Closed: Inputs are carefully controlled.	Open: We are provided a rich variety of inputs ("immersions").
Serial-processed: All learners are expected to follow the same learning sequence; learners only learn one thing at a time.	Parallel-processed: Different learners simultaneously follow different learning paths; many types of learning happen at the same time for individual learners.
Designed: Both knowledge and the learning process are predetermined by others.	Emergent: Knowledge is created through the relationships between the knower and the known. The outcome cannot be known in advance.
Controlled: The "teacher" determines what, when, and how we learn.	Self-organized: We are active in the design of curriculum, activities, and assessment; teacher is a facilitator and designer of learning.
Discrete, separated: Disciplines are separate and independent; roles of teacher and student clearly differentiated.	Messy, webbed: Disciplines are integrated; roles are flexible.
Static: Same material and method applied to all students.	Adaptive: Material and teaching methods vary based on our interests and learning styles.
Linear: Material is taught in predictable, controlled sequences, from simple "parts" to complex "wholes."	Nonlinear: We learn nonsequentially, with rapid and frequent iteration between parts and wholes.
Competing: We learn alone and compete with others for rewards.	Co-evolving: We learn together; our "intelligence" is based on our learning community.

From: Cleveland, J. (1995, March 22–24). The changing nature of learning. Background information for the Community Learning Enterprise design workshop.

- E-portfolios

- Group and/or individual projects

- Written case studies

- Concept papers and maps

- Surveys

- Field experiences

- Short quizzes

- Proctored exams at local sites

- Video conferencing

- Voicemail

I conducted telephone and email inquires regarding the assessment practices of community colleges. Seven colleges were selected to provide a fresh look at current assessment practices and behaviors of colleges in urban and rural communities, colleges involved in the developmental stage of assessment planning, and colleges serving large numbers of minority students. The inquiries confirmed community colleges' steadfast and unrelenting efforts to ensure quality and successful outcomes for their students. The following examples are listed to highlight the various methods used in community colleges to assess the learning of students engaged in online course instruction.

San Diego Community College District

Gin Gee, a professor at the San Diego Community College District, believes strongly in pre-assessing his students to ensure a greater likelihood for their success. Otherwise, he maintains, time is wasted and accidents may occur with experiments as the result of poor performance.

Students enrolled in the Principles of Biology Lab are required to read the "Hands-on Experiment" and complete the Readiness Assessment Test (RAT). The pre-assessment requires students to gather materials and supplies for the experiment. Dr. Gee asks for a digital photo to document their readiness for conducting the experiment.

Weekly biology experiments are evaluated on the clarity of instructions and content. This assessment is particularly useful to Dr. Gee for

experimental protocols and helps to provide input for continual improvement and fine-tuning the course.

Dr. Gee also evaluates student lab reports that are required to be
uploaded onto the course web site. The reports are graded on quality,
completeness, and critical thinking demonstrated by the student's interpretation, analysis, and discussion of the assignment. The report contains
experiment results that are presented in graphs or tables, diagrams, and
other media—very rich resources for assessment.

A midterm, final exam, and weekly group discussion on the electronic
discussion board also evaluate student performance. Once a student com-
pletes Dr. Gee's course, they are required to complete a Course Evaluation
and Student Feedback Survey.

Kirkwood Community College

Michele Payne, director of learning initiatives, reports that all courses and
programs at Kirkwood Community College are reviewed on a regular
basis: vocational classes are reviewed by the program review committee
and the state; liberal arts courses are reviewed by the curriculum and
instruction committee at the college. Completion rates serve as an indicator of success.

The college encourages its faculty to consider the self-review developed by the Michigan Cooperative that presents various aspects of online
course design and their effect on student achievement.

Edison Community College

Ann Miller, the Internet instructional administrator at Edison Community College (ECC), agrees with Taylor (2002) that "Assessment is something everybody struggles with" (p. 10). She reports that in the assessment
process, someone other than the student registered for the course could sit
in for the exam, texts and other sources of assistance could be used in completing exams, and technical difficulties could occur during the exam.

ECC has initiated a number of approaches to dissuade these situations
by expecting students to take tests in the learning center staffed by proctors,
placing limits on the time allotted to complete an exam online, giving
open-book tests, and assessing student grades by assigning a grade for the
level of class participation and completed portfolios. One faculty member
has changed his thinking about testing, viewing it as a learning process. He

allows students to take the exam more than once and calculates 50% of the grade on tests and 50% on student participation (Taylor, 2002).

Cowley County Community College

Instructors use a variety of assessment techniques, including multiple-choice exams and essays. Biology classes are designed to conduct experiments at home and require traditional lab reports. The astronomy class engages in field trips and requires group and/or individual reports. Exams are administered online and/or proctored on site. Cowley County Community College (CCCC) utilizes the management and assessment tools offered by WebCT, which, they report, allows for building a strong sense of classroom community among online learners.

The online program at CCCC has enjoyed rapid growth and acceptance since its inception in fall 2000. The college administers student surveys and reports high levels of satisfaction for online learning. In the last report in spring 2003, 90% of the students responding reported that they would either "Almost Always" or "Frequently" recommend their online class to other students, and retention and satisfaction remain high.

El Paso Community College

The mission of El Paso Community College (EPCC) is to provide the opportunity for affordable, quality education for everyone in its service area and to remain sensitive to the educational needs of area employers by providing the necessary training to support the needs of the workforce community. "El Paso Community College takes very seriously the goal of matching the technical needs of area employers with our current curriculum offerings" (Canales, 2003, p. 3).

Based on student retention rates that were less than acceptable, EPCC recognized that it was time to take major steps to ensure quality and success with its online students. This resulted in the Instructional Technology Master Plan, originally developed in 1996, that is scrutinized annually and designed to bridge efforts into the 21st century. (The entire document may be found on the EPCC intranet: http://www.epcc.edu/IT/IT_MASTER_PLAN_2004.pps.) An excerpt from the section on assessment is below.

- Teachers are expected to select assessment techniques that are consistent with the objectives of their course.

- Assessment procedures and grading standards are communicated clearly to students at the beginning of the course.

- Students are provided prompt and accurate feedback on their performance of exams, papers, and assignments and at regular intervals throughout the course.

- An explanation is provided on "how" student work is graded.

- Students are given constructive suggestions on how to improve their course grade.

- The college uses data to drive its techniques and strategies used for assessment.

Teachers are expected to select techniques that are reliable, valid, and consistent with course objectives. These points become questionable when a student is graded on skills that are not part of the announced course objectives and/or were not given adequate preparation and practice opportunities during the course. EPCC contends that another violation of valid assessment occurs when faculty members teaching two different sections of the same course use drastically different assessment procedures or grading standards (Canales, 2003).

EPCC maintains a strong commitment to student success and quality instruction and promotes faculty development, institutional support systems, mentors, comprehensive orientation for online students, and ongoing, campus-wide tweaking of the existing technology plan.

Iowa Central Community College

In 1994, Iowa Central Community College instituted a strategic planning process and expanded the plan in 1998, using its original practices, which included collaboration, cross-functional teams, financial support, multiple measures of student learning, and a means to assess student learning—the college's central focus. The college has assigned a curriculum and instruction council and an assessment team to oversee the progress of assessment in each department of the college included in the annual report.

Students are made aware of the assessment process at the start of classes. All departments are required to submit an assessment report for each course taught in the department (see Table 1.2).

Table 1.2

Course-Level Assessment

Course	Assessment Method	Result	Action
For any course	List of evaluation methods such as tests/quizzes, comprehensive finals, departmental exams, labs, written reports, oral presentations, projects, portfolios, journals, peer evaluations, self-evaluations, computer, homework	Identify problem areas	Modify instructional materials/methods/curriculum as necessary; make budgetary recommendations; make planning recommendations

At this time, instructors use the same course syllabus and evaluation tools for Internet classes; however, two evaluation options are offered to students taking Internet classes.

- *Option 1.* The exam is offered online, the student is required to have a password to begin, the exam is timed, and the instructor sets the time limit. This option is used 99% of the time.

- *Option 2.* The exam is proctored and taken at a local, approved testing site. Exams are sent to the proctor, the instructor determines where the exam is to be returned, and exams are stored in a locked, secured environment. Students must present a student photo ID before a test is administered.

Data show no significant difference in the success of students choosing face-to-face classes as compared to students taking classes via the Internet (see Table 1.3; Iowa Central Community College, 2002).

Paducah Community College

Providing its community of learners with distance education is no new task for Paducah Community College (PCC). PCC has been offering distance-learning courses via televised video since 1976, interactive television courses since 1990, computer-mediated courses since 1991, and web-based courses since 1996. Traditional methods have been used for assessment: student evaluation of instruction, surveys, and analysis of grade distribution and attrition rates.

Table 1.3

GPA Comparison of Face-to-Face and Internet Classes

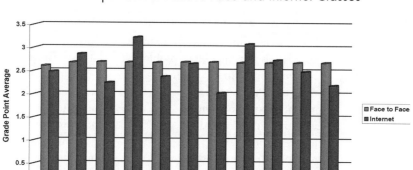

Student evaluation of instruction. PCC believes this to be the strongest indicator of course quality. The traditional evaluation was adapted for use with distance learners and is accessible online and readily made available to division chairs, program coordinators, and the like. The form is continually updated to reflect changes. Responses to the evaluation serve the college well, especially with regard to an instructor's understanding of technology-related demands, the number of times a student is in contact with the instructor, and the quality of those contacts.

Surveys. The survey responses reveal if students feel they are receiving an education equal to that of an on-campus course, the level at which they are performing technologically, the level of discussion that needs to occur between faculty and other students, and if students feel they are given adequate information to perform the requirements of the class. Other useful information from the surveys provides data on the success rates, reasons for incompletes, and suggestions for improvement. The college has found these surveys to be exceptionally useful in program development and in organizing coordinated efforts between departments.

Grade distribution. While distribution of grades does not specifically address whether students are learning, it can be used to complement other factors like task performance.

Attrition rate. Attrition rates in and of themselves cannot tell the whole story, but using the information in combination with other inquiries can provide significant and useful guidance for improvement and/or change.

PCC adopted a careful screening and selection process for students enrolling in distance-learning courses. Students must demonstrate that they possess attributes that make them better candidates for success, such as being self-starters, having self-discipline, possessing knowledge of the technology required in the course, and having the ability to meet faculty and students in a virtual environment.

The very mode of communication, that is, email communication, provides concrete and recorded evidence of student learning, such as progression in grammar, organization, and development. Threaded discussion provides evidence by analyzing the change in the level of questions and responses by each individual student. Indeed, the written communication provides a permanent record of accomplishment and growth—or none.

Moreover, exchanging ideas, typically referred to as branching ideas, provides the instructor with a better understanding of the level at which a student is comprehending concepts and offers evidence as to whether monitoring and/or adjustment is required (Wade, 1999).

PREVENTION CAN BE A CURE

Most, if not all, community colleges across our nation have technology plans that are ever-changing documents that include strategies and techniques striving to prepare students adequately so that they might enjoy success through distance-learning courses. The following presents useful suggestions about what instructors can do to help students succeed in distance education.

- Teach students about the special instructional features of the program, such as glossaries, self-tests, multimedia material, and supplementary information.

- Teach them how to USE the special instructional features of the program.

- Teach students about the special technical tools available, such as chat rooms, contacting the instructor, and getting help.

- Teach them how to USE the special technical tools.

- Provide instruction in critical self-regulation areas, such as time management, flexibility of time and location, generating and maintaining motivation, self-testing, and managing anxiety.

- Help students develop a management plan to successfully complete the course that includes goals, personal resources required to reach the goals, a plan to reach each goal, methods to accomplish their plan, implementing the plan, monitoring the success and timeliness of the plan, formatively evaluating their progress, modifying methods and/or goals, and summatively evaluating the outcomes to determine if the plan is to be used again, revised, or discarded.

  (Weinstein, Corliss, Cho, & Bera, 2002, pp. 1–2)

Assessing student online learning is in its infancy. Many colleges have adapted traditional strategies as a launching-pad effort to assess student learning. Whatever the strategy, protocol, process, or technique, let us remember the great advantages and learning opportunities for students engaged in the journey of online course instruction.

- Students are engaged in time-on-task activities to get the work done.

- There is a permanent record of student work that is always available for review by the instructor and the student.

- Students are engaged in collaborative learning communities that build and strengthen skills commanded by today's workforce.

- Students and instructors are meeting one another more frequently and getting to know one another on deeper levels.

- Students, fellow students, and instructors remain constantly engaged with one another.

- Students are reading and attending to assignments regularly.

- Students are experiencing more writing in all disciplines, and writing is not restricted to a handful of courses.

- Students are organizing thoughts and responding continuously with instructors and fellow students.

- Students are assessing, thinking, reflecting, and responding with more frequency.

These factors do not consider the skill sets that accompany students as they register for online instruction—advanced skills including computer jargon, navigation, and the like.

Based on the information gathered for this chapter, in all likelihood, Bloom (1956) would be encouraged by the domains (cognitive, affective, and psychomotor) affected in students who matriculate from online instruction because of the practices, behaviors, and activities that require their regular engagement and response.

This chapter also offers evidence to support and encourage community college professionals about the aggressive actions taken by community colleges in our nation to ensure quality instruction and assessment of student learning for students who register for online courses. I am certain that, with their history of ingenuity and resiliency, community colleges are strong contenders as providers in the delivery of online instruction and learning for 21st-century students.

2

Designing and Managing Student Assessment in an Online Learning Environment

Mahnaz Moallem

Several years ago, before online learning became a formal instructional delivery system, I went through a major pedagogical change in my teaching practice. When I first began changing my teaching style from a teacher-centered, test-based, outcome-based approach to a more student-centered, process-based, problem-based, or project-based approach (Sanders, 2001), I had to develop a new conceptual framework for thinking about teaching and learning. Through reflection and analysis of my practice, I realized that my success in encouraging active learning and growth toward self-directed learning, in allowing students to define their own learning tasks, in facilitating group learning, and in ensuring student knowledge and application was very dependent on my assessment system.

In the following sections:

- I reflect on my student-centered, project-based assessment system and share some of the implementation problems that I encountered.

- I explain how these experiences influenced my thinking about an online learning environment and its assessment system.

- I describe my design framework for the assessment of my online courses and provide details of the process of designing, developing, and implementing such design.

- I share some of the barriers and enablers that I found, and the lessons that I learned.

FROM A TEST-BASED TO A PROJECT-BASED ASSESSMENT SYSTEM: A REFLECTION ON PRACTICE

Changing from an assessment system primarily focused on outcomes and consisting of infrequent tests and papers to an ongoing assessment system focused on the process and outcomes of learning (Biggs, 1996) was both challenging and exciting. The challenge of creating a system that intertwined teaching and assessment was conceptual as well as experiential. I wanted my new teaching strategies to encourage authentic learning, provide diverse learning opportunities for critical thinking skills and greater depth of knowledge, develop a deeper dialogue over the course of material, and foster both individual and group-oriented learning activities. Accordingly, these teaching methods required a dynamic, continuous, and performance-based assessment system that emphasized progress in learning and in becoming increasingly sophisticated learners and knowers (Huba & Freed, 2000). Creating, sustaining, and assessing such quality learning experiences required a new conceptual framework (see Figure 2.1) and time to experiment with the ideas and learn from the practice.

Figure 2.1

Student-Centered, Performance-Based, Process-Based Assessment Model

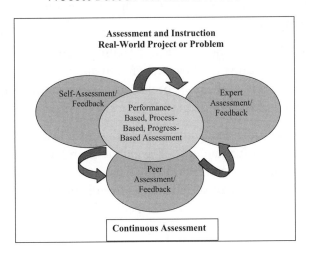

Regardless of the challenges, the student-centered, performance-based approach to teaching and assessment was very exciting because it involved gathering information from a variety of sources to cultivate a rich and meaningful understanding of student learning (Travis, 1996). This approach to learning provides opportunities for students to use their knowledge to perform specific and realistic tasks. It also makes it essential for me to provide timely and constructive feedback to help students have the time to make the necessary changes in their work before turning in their next assignment. Such feedback is intended to help the student assess his or her strengths and weaknesses, identifying areas of needed growth and mobilizing current capacity.

Despite many opportunities that the performance-based, project- or problem-based assessment system provided, there were several implementation and management problems that hindered the effectiveness of this system in a traditional face-to-face classroom. The following summarizes the major implementation and management problems.

- While the concept of dynamic and continuous assessment was appealing and made integration of assessment and instruction possible, monitoring and documenting students' progress in order to provide timely and formative feedback was very difficult to manage.

- It seemed that limitation of time, tools, and resources for gathering and documenting day-to-day assessment data constrained the effectiveness of authentic assessment and problem-based or project-based learning. Teacher periodic observation and anecdotal notes as tools to document the process of learning did not seem to be effective data-gathering tools.

- It was difficult to be an effective facilitator and to ask appropriate guiding questions to allow students to approach progressively the solution to the problem or project at hand without adequate documentation of student progress.

- Promoting individual students' growth was difficult without providing individual (private) as well as public (team) assessment activities. Nevertheless, providing individual assessment activities tended to change the nature of such activities from being self-assessment tools for improvement to formal assessment of learning.

- Developing self-assessment tools and checklists was difficult and required time to develop and test. However, in practice such tools did not seem to work effectively without the instructor's feedback and guidance. Furthermore, it was difficult to document the effects of self-assessment tools on individual growth and team performance.

- Using multiple sources of assessment information—multiple measures of learning that assess different types (declarative, structural, procedural) and level of knowledge acquisition—was difficult to manage given the limitation of time and resources.

In spite of the above challenges, anchoring all learning activities to a larger project or problem and assessing students' learning outcomes by directly observing their performance in a real-world project is very rewarding and successful. Regular face-to-face meetings with students as they work on their projects combined with self-assessment checklists and rubrics provide an excellent environment for students to demonstrate their ability to apply their knowledge in real-world environments. Meeting with students as they develop their products makes the formative nature of feedback more effective and more of a two-way system. In other words, regular meetings help students see the gaps between their performance and the standards we set as the best performance. Students then revise their work addressing the issues and gaps we identify. As many scholars who advocate authentic and performance-based assessment observe (Harp, 1991), one of the premises of project-based, or performance-based, authentic assessment is its equal focus on both continuous and individualized assessment.

In summary, even though developing performance-based projects and then coaching and guiding students as they completed their projects was challenging and time-consuming it was also very fulfilling and encouraging. As students began to see their learning products and realized how much they had learned and how well they were able to transfer their knowledge to the real-world environment, their motivation and feeling of satisfaction improved.

In the following section I explain how my experiences with a performance-based assessment system in face-to-face classrooms influenced my thinking about online learning and its assessment system.

A PERFORMANCE-BASED ASSESSMENT SYSTEM
IN AN ONLINE LEARNING ENVIRONMENT

When I first began thinking about the online learning environment and exploring the course management systems, one area that excited me was the potential of online courses for assessment of the learning process and application of the student-centered teaching and learning approach. This potential, combined with the result of literature review that indicates online learning environments have the highest potential for real world, authentic performance assessment (e.g., Hazari & Schno, 1999; Nelson, 1998; Wild & Omari, 1996), convinced me to apply my new pedagogy of teaching and assessment to an online learning environment.

Reviewing available course management systems (e.g., WebCT, Blackboard) for online delivery of instruction suggested that there are several tools and resources within this technology that are not readily available in face-to-face instruction. Such tools and resources seem to provide an easier and more effective system to conduct project-based assessment because of their emphasis on interactive, formative, and continuous assessment. Some of these tools and resources are as follows.

- The database and interactive system to track, monitor, and document students' activities automatically

- Easy access and an easy development process for conventional assessment tools (quizzes, open-ended questions, etc.) to give students the opportunity to self-assess their own knowledge through automatic and instant feedback

- Multiple communication tools to facilitate and to document dialogue between and among learners, materials, and the instructor

- Content tools to develop projects and problem-solving tasks that could incorporate multiple resources and perspectives and be completed at various intervals

- Communication and content tools to provide continuous formal and informal feedback on assignments, thoughts, and progress from both the instructor and peers and other mentors or colleagues

- Unlimited and self-paced access to course materials and communication tools to complete independent and team work projects/problems at any time

- Interactive but asynchronous communication tools to promote thoughtful and reflective commentaries

- Both learner and instructor access to the record of responses, answers, and feedback to analyze and interpret one's own performance and to reflect

In addition to the availability of these assessment tools and resources, online teaching and learning seems to provide a much better environment for practicing duties of a mentor or facilitator. Given automatic documentation of student work as well as easy access to such records, providing proper guidance and feedback is not as difficult as it is in traditional face-to-face classrooms.

Because online learning environments, by their nature, provide more learner control, I needed to have a more specific plan as to how different forms of assessment should be integrated into the course design.

A MODEL FOR ASSESSMENT OF ONLINE LEARNING

Figure 2.2 shows my new conceptualization of project-based assessment in an online learning environment. As Figure 2.2 shows, a challenging, complex, and authentic task, project, or investigation is the main focus of assessment of student learning. Such a task bears a close relationship to real-world problems in the home and workplace of today and tomorrow and involves sustained amounts of time to be completed. This larger and more ambitious project/problem is divided into smaller tasks that prepare students for the larger and more complex tasks. The assessment of projects is integrated in instruction and occurs throughout the instruction. However, as Figure 2.2 shows, three stages of assessment can coexist for each task regardless of its complexity in an online learning environment. These stages include initial assessment, progress assessment, and product assessment. While each stage of assessment has different purposes, the process and results of each assessment stage affect other stages directly. In all stages of assessment, students take charge and are involved in setting and using standards of excellence to evaluate whether they have achieved their goals. In each stage of assessment, the teacher/expert monitors individual students as they work on instructional tasks in order to assess thinking processes and provide ongoing feedback. Projects and other instructional tasks are designed to be completed by groups, and students are encouraged to not only share ideas and resources but also to assess each other's work. Thus, for each instructional task three different, but related, assessment tools are used: self-assessment, expert assessment, and peer assessment. During all stages of assessment, the feedback provided by the instructor and peers is meant to be formative; that is, it is intended to help the student assess his or her strengths and weaknesses, identify areas of needed growth, and mobilize current capacity. Performances become tools for reflection on learning accomplished and learning deferred.

Figure 2.2

A Model for Assessment of Online Learning

Continuous Assessment of Learning and Instruction

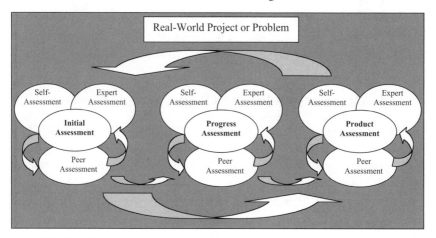

Stages of Online Assessment

The *initial assessment* stage provides both public and private assessment activities in which individual learners test their current knowledge constructions and understanding before having to work with groups or go public with their ideas. During this stage the teacher/expert reviews the student's initial thoughts and provides individual and private feedback to foster further thinking and reflection. After self-reflection and self-assessment of initial thoughts, the learner goes public by sharing his/her ideas with peers or group members. This initial sharing of ideas provides an opportunity for the student to benefit from peers' perspectives. By focusing attention on the contrast between what the student generated and what other peers thought of the product, the student then engages in more self-assessment and may begin noticing important distinctions among different perspectives and accommodating new ideas (Schwartz & Bransford, 1998).

During the stage of *progress assessment,* students will work as teams to share and discuss ideas, consult resources, listen and read just-in-time lectures, and explore ways to solve the problem in hand. The teacher/expert's role is critical as students try to solve the problem. The teacher/expert should closely monitor the teams' discussions and individual student contributions in order to provide new resources or redirect students to the existing resources, offer just-in-time lectures or skill-building lessons, ask guiding questions, and help students test their thoughts or solutions using self-assessment rubrics or criteria. During this stage the three forms of assessment—self-assessment, peer assessment, and expert assessment—may occur all at the same time. As a result of working with teams, which involves peer discussion and peer assessment, individual students may engage in self-assessment of their own thoughts and ideas. They may realize the needs for seeking more information, exploring extra resources, and mastering areas of knowledge and skills that are lacking. The teacher/expert's continuous assessment of the teams' progress toward their goals should provide a different level of assessment for both teams and individual students. Therefore, the combination of self-assessment, peer assessment, and expert assessment during the process of solving problems should help students to progress in their thinking and in solving the bigger problem or project.

The last stage of assessment—*product assessment*—occurs at three levels. Individual students and teams should use both the standards and criteria for the best product to conduct a self-assessment of their own products and identify the needed areas of improvement. Teams may serve as peer reviewers of each other's products and provide constructive feedback. The teacher/expert's periodic review of students' products should also provide formative information about the quality of the final product. As a result of this multiple level of formative assessment, the quality of students' final products should be assured. The summative evaluation of students' products should serve as a means of both evaluating achievements of goals and the effectiveness of instruction.

APPLYING CONTINUOUS ASSESSMENT OF LEARNING AND INSTRUCTION MODEL IN THE DESIGN OF ONLINE COURSES

I used the continuous assessment of learning and instruction model to design and develop the assessment system for two graduate-level courses I regularly teach in instructional design and development. I used the WebCT course management system as the primary platform for designing and delivering the courses. For each course, I developed a real-world problem or project that requires students to demonstrate achievement of all course goals and objectives and make it the focal point and the main requirement for completion of the course (see Table 2.1 for an example).

Table 2.1
Examples of Course Projects

MIT 500: Instructional Systems Design:
Theory and Research Course Project

- **Instructional Material:** Students will design, develop, and evaluate an instructional module using instructional design principles as their major framework and a specific instructional theory as their module design model (**click here for examples**). The instructional module should be self-instructional and should not require more than 45 minutes to complete. Students are free to select the instructional topic. (It is strongly suggested that students work with a client to identify a topic that is one of the client's interests). The instructional module may use any media as appropriate. Media options may include a slide/tape presentation, printed workbook, a videotape, or a web-based lesson, among other options. When developing the module, keep in mind that the emphasis of this course is on instructional design principles rather than on media production techniques. The focus is on stating instructional goals, deriving appropriate instructional content, making the instruction appropriate for the audience, and developing appropriate instructional strategies. The emphasis is not on the artistic quality of the materials. **Click here** to review descriptions of instructional materials/products. **Click here** to review the tips for developing the instructional materials and writing product reports. (**90 points**)

- **Product Report:** In addition to the copy of the developed product, each student (or team) must prepare a written report no longer than 10 pages that provides evidence of the analysis, design, development, and evaluation of the instructional material. (Evaluation should include both one-on-one and small group). You may choose the format of the report. However, the report should include an executive summary; a section on the theoretical orientation and a rationale for the applied design model; a section on goals, objectives, assessment, and sequence of the materials; and a section on evaluation plan, implementation of the evaluation plan, and a summary of the results. The 10-page limit refers to the body of the paper; appendices may create a longer product report. Appendices should include the analysis documentation (e.g., questionnaire, interview, etc.), evaluation documentation (e.g., formative evaluation data, revisions made, etc.), a log of the hours spent on different aspects of the project, minutes from meetings with the client, and evaluation documents. Your report must be professional (carefully edited and formatted). See **Product Report** for more information. Also see the **timeline for completing the product and the product reports.** (**90 points**)

The project is complex and multifaceted and requires students to engage in activities which present the same type of cognitive challenges as those in the real world (Honebein, Duffy, & Fishman, 1993). In addition, in order to complete the project, students work in teams and with real clients and/or the professional community and develop their products for delivery in these environments. The complexity of the project and its relatively long-term integrated units of instruction make it necessary to break the task into several subtasks or mini projects to be completed at various intervals (see Table 2.2 for an example).

Table 2.2

Example of Subtasks or Mini Projects

Report I	Report I (Due October 31)
Section 1: Assumptions	Report I, Section 1: Summary of Theoretical Assumptions
Section 2: Instructional Goal(s)	**Part 1:** Given that you use the general instructional systems design model as your overall design framework, explain which specific instructional model you use to design and deliver your lesson(s). Be specific when describing the components of your lesson(s) and how you have applied the theory into the lesson design.
Section 3: Task Analysis	
Section 4: Analysis of Learner and Learning Context	**Parts 2 & 3:** In this part you should present information that is derived principally from learner and situation analysis. The purpose of this section is to inform me about those characteristics and attributes that you have found about the learners and instructional setting that are reflected in your lesson(s). Traditionally, information about the learners
Scoring Sheet	includes a description of the learner's entry behaviors (prereq-

Report II

Section 1: Objectives, Assessment, Strategies

Scoring Sheet

Report III

Section 1: Results of Evaluation

Section 2: Planning and Time Log

Scoring Sheet

Appendices

uisites) and the rationale for including them, and general characteristics of learners and the relationship between the identified characteristics and the instruction provided.

Report I, Section 2: Instructional Goal(s)

Part 1: The instructional goal(s) for the module/unit should be identified and stated in terms of the learner's learning outcome. The primary consideration in the selection of the general goal for your module or instructional material is that you do not select a topic area which will require many hours of instruction. A general guideline is to select something which would normally require about 45 minutes of typical classroom time to teach. If your target population is young children, you should consider something which requires even less time. Adult materials might extend one and one-half hours. Keep in mind that the material you are developing should not be led by an instructor, but should be designed as self-instructional material.

These time parameters are suggested in order to limit the amount of work you will be required to do in developing, evaluating, and revising your instruction, as well as to limit the time required for students to participate in the formative evaluation process. A second consideration is the selection of a topic. If you are working with a client (a professor, trainer, etc.), make sure you check the content of your lesson with the content expert regularly. If you are not working with a client, select a topic with which you are already familiar . . .

MIT 500: Product Report: Components Descriptions

This strategy helps provide structure and serves as a timeline for student work as well as incorporates process-based, continuous assessment and feedback. The project description and a detailed list of processes and timeline for completion are linked to the course home page, course lessons/modules, course syllabus, and course calendar. To make it possible for students to self-assess their own products and for peer reviewers and the instructor to have a clear list of assessment criteria, I developed a series of self-assessment rubrics for the project (see Table 2.3 for an example) and linked the rubrics to the project description site. One or two completed projects are also linked to the course project to help students set the standards for their performances.

Table 2.3

Example of a Self-Assessment Instrument

Description of Report I	H	M	L	Total
Section 1: Theoretical Assumptions *Part 1: Instructional Model* • Your adopted model is described and provides specific information about the components of the model				5
Part 2: Learner and Context Analysis *1) Provides detailed analysis of the learner* • Described learner's entry behavior (prerequisites) • Described learner's prior knowledge • Described general characteristics of the learner (attitude, learning preferences, etc.) • Described data sources and analysis techniques *2) Provides detailed analysis of the learning context* • Described physical aspects of the site • Described social aspects of the site				10
Section 2: Goal Statement • Provided a clear description of instructional goal(s) • Identified the subgoals and stated them in terms of the learner's learning outcome • Accurately identified the learning domains and categories of learning outcomes for each goal statement				5
Section 3: Task Analysis • Conducted goal/task analysis for the instructional goal(s) • Showed in the goal/task analysis flowchart the main steps (subskills) • Showed in the goal/task analysis flowchart the entry behaviors				10
Predicated Total Score				
What did you find as strengths of your work? **What did you find as weaknesses of your work?** **How can you improve your work?**				

In order to provide online space for students to work on their course project continuously and in collaboration with their team members throughout the semester, I set up the Student Presentations area within WebCT course management system. Student Presentations allows the course designer to create groups of students within a class and assign them a project that they assemble in their own area of WebCT. Within the Student Presentations area, group members could collaboratively develop and work on a project and use the internal mail system and specific discussion area to communicate with one another, the instructor, and possible guest members. The instructor and the peer reviewers also use the Student Presentations area to provide feedback and guidance as needed.

My next step in designing the performance assessment system was to develop related problems or cases for each unit of instruction in order to provide the required learning experiences for the completion of the course project. Each case, its resources, and supporting instructional materials are clustered together to form a unit of instruction. I used the WebCT content module to organize and develop units. Within each unit students are directed to work as teams to solve the unit's case or problem. I developed a list of thinking questions (see Table 2.4 for an example) for each unit that

Table 2.4

Example of Thinking Questions

Summary Questions 1
Due January 16 (by midnight)
I Purpose I Direction I Required Readings I Summary Questions
How to Submit

Summary Questions: Prepare a written answer to the following Summary Questions and submit it by January 16 no later than 12:00 a.m.

1) How is instructional systems design different from traditional curriculum development? What is your reaction to the differences?

2) What is systems approach to instruction (general systems theory) and how is it being applied in instructional design models/conceptual frameworks and principles? How would you evaluate this approach for designing a curriculum?

How to Submit: *Submit your summary by January 16* no later than 12:00 a.m. To submit your summary click on the **Quiz** link at the end of the **Action Menu** row of links above at the top of this page.

---

encourages individual students to activate their prior knowledge and to make their implicit thoughts explicit. Students use the Assignments area to respond to these questions before they begin working with their teams. I review each student's response and offer feedback and comments that focus on fostering thinking and promoting student's self-reflection. For each unit, I also developed nongraded, self-assessment quizzes with immediate feedback using the WebCT Quiz Maker so students can assess their understanding of the reading materials before engaging in any forms of discussion.

As students begin working as teams, I suggest that each team member present his or her initial thoughts about the case. The purpose of initial sharing is to help individual students compare and contrast their own thoughts with their peers' thoughts and begin to accommodate new ideas. It also helps me examine and track the progress in individuals' thoughts and provide private feedback as needed. I developed team-assessment criteria and rubrics (Table 2.5 shows one example of student team assessment rubric) to help teams assess their own performance and the final team products. Upon completion of each problem-solving task, team recorders are expected to post the team's final response/solution/product in the Forum area. As a class, we review each team's response to the problem at hand. As an instructor, I also provide elaborate feedback and suggestions for improvement to each team.

While none of these units' related activities were formally graded, I assign a participation grade for both individual assignments and team activities based on a set of criteria which the class develops. These strategies help students focus more on the formative nature of assessment tools and they use the results to improve their learning.

REFLECTIONS AND CONCLUSION

I strongly believe that online learning environments facilitate application of dynamic, performance-based, process- and product-based methods and approaches to assessment. As many scholars observed (i.e., Oliver, 2000), this new assessment system has potential to motivate students and promote more effective online learning. However, several overall barriers that may impede the successful implementation of such online assessment systems must be removed from the process. These barriers can be summarized as follows: accessibility and responsiveness of the instructor,

Table 2.5

An Example of a Team Assessment Rubric

We have used the following evaluation rubric to assess our team's performance.

4—Thorough Understanding

- Every member consistently and actively works toward group goals.
- Every member is sensitive to the feelings and learning needs of all group members.
- Every member willingly accepts and fulfills his or her individual role within the group.
- Every member consistently and actively contributes knowledge, opinions, and skills.
- Every member values the knowledge, opinion, and skills of all group members and encourages their contribution.
- Every member helps the group identify necessary changes and encourages group action for change.

3—Good Understanding

- Every member works toward group goals without prompting.
- Every member accepts and fulfills his or her individual role within the group.
- Every member contributes knowledge, opinions, and skills without prompting.
- Every member shows sensitivity to the feelings of others.
- Every member willingly participates in needed changes.

2—Satisfactory Understanding

- Every member works toward group goals with occasional prompting.
- Every member contributes to the group with occasional prompting.
- Every member shows sensitivity to the feelings of others.
- Every member participates in needed changes, with occasional prompting.

1—Needs Improvement

- Every member works toward group goals only when prompted.
- Every member contributes to the group only when prompted.
- Every member needs occasional reminders to be sensitive to the feelings of others.
- Every member participates in needed changes when prompted and encouraged.

instructor's philosophy of learning and assessment and his or her expectations of students, and fostering a participatory online learning environment. Despite the development time it took for me to design and implement these assessment tools and the time and effort it takes to have students use these assessment tools to monitor their own progress, it proved worth the effort.

Implementing dynamic, performance-based, process-based assessment in an online learning environment provides several opportunities.

- Dynamic, performance-based, process-based online assessment systems make assessment a natural extension of instruction rather than the end process.

- The online, dynamic, performance-based assessment techniques are nongraded, reusable, and part of instructional activities that provide both the students and instructor with useful feedback on the teaching-learning process.

- Since assessment in this schematic becomes a constant feedback, it enables students to be strategic in their own learning process and enables the instructor to adapt the instructional process to meet student needs.

- Assessment of actual performance enables students to translate what they learn in different units of instruction to real-life applications.

- In the online, dynamic, performance-based, process-based assessment system it is possible to provide a wide range of assessment tools and techniques.

- The online, dynamic, performance-based, process-based assessment system offers more opportunities and ways for providing feedback.

- The online, dynamic, performance-based, process-based assessment system makes the management, collection, and transfer of assessment information possible.

- The online, dynamic, performance-based, process-based assessment system involves students in developing the process that leads to the final product.

3

Team Assessment Guidelines: A Case Study of Collaborative Learning in Design

Karen Belfer
Ron Wakkary

The main objective of collaborative learning is for learners to work together and share knowledge, yet still stand separately as an individual learner, withstand the whims of group dynamics, and not lose the joy of group learning due to the administration of the learning task. In order to successfully implement constructivist learning activities, Morrison (2003) describes the need for the developers (e.g., instructional designer, subject matter expert, instructor) to translate the principles of constructivism, their values, and assumptions of teaching and learning into effective practice strategies. We would add to this the means to address the learning goals and the characteristics of learners. Equally, in regard to teamwork assessment, the components of learning design, environment, and evaluation must all work together within the course design, development, and delivery. We believe that effective assessment of collaborative work requires the interweaving of the assessment of learning standards with sound instructional design decisions, sensible use and understanding of constructivist approaches (Belfer & Wakkary, 2002).

In this chapter, we provide a case study analysis of the design and implementation of a collaborative learning assessment methodology within an interaction design course utilizing a mixed-mode model of face-to-face and online learning. In harmony with program level goals, the desired learning strategies and goals of the course include learning effectiveness, learner centeredness, responsiveness to workplace needs, and effective use of educational technology. We will evaluate the effectiveness of team assessment within the case study using guidelines we developed.

In order to describe the use and value of the suggested guidelines,

- We provide an introduction of our guidelines for effective team assessment.

- We present our case study, which includes a description of the course and a detailed description of the learning and assessment methods employed.

- We provide an analysis and diagnosis of the case study utilizing our Team Assessment Guidelines Checklist.

- We conclude with recommendations for the design and implementation of these strategies and the potential use of the checklist in other courses.

GUIDELINES FOR ASSESSMENT

We developed a two-tier (at the course and at the activity level) approach that takes into account the values of cooperative learning and a framework that supports good instructional design, providing developers and instructors with guidelines that enable sound team assessment practices. In the following segments we describe why we considered instructional design, the principles of cooperative learning, peer and self-assessment, and the assessment of learning to be the core elements addressed by our team assessment guidelines.

Instructional Design

Instructional design is a systematic approach to curriculum and course development that focuses on learning objectives as a means for the development of learning experiences. These objectives are based on the learners' characteristics, and associated with other units, segments, and courses that are part of the curriculum. The learning objectives communicate the knowledge and skills learners can expect as outcomes of the completed unit of study. They give purpose to instruction and should be adopted as the focus for the design of learning activities, experiences, materials, assessments, and feedback techniques, and seen as an inherent part of the educational structure seeking to provide consistency amongst all.

To justify the development of collaborative activities that include team assessment, we would expect to find great cohesiveness among the learner characteristics, the course objectives, and the selected learning approach.

Principles of Cooperative Learning

The purpose behind collaborative learning is to design activities that motivate learners to work with each other and to see the value of sharing their views and knowledge. No matter what methodology one uses, it is important to follow the principles of cooperative learning.

Educational research points to five essential elements that make cooperative learning activities work.

- *Positive interdependence.* Students need to perceive that they need each other in order to be able to complete the group's task.

- *Individual accountability.* Students should be responsible for their own learning and be able to perform at a comparable level with or without their team.

- *Promoting interaction.* Students promote each other's learning by helping, sharing, and encouraging efforts to learn.

- *Team skills.* For a team to function effectively, its members need to use and practice leadership, decision-making, trust-building, communication, and conflict-management skills.

- *Group processing.* Groups need specific time to discuss how well they are achieving their goals and maintaining effective working relationships among members.

(Johnson, Johnson, & Holubec, 1993)

The principles of positive interdependence and individual accountability have major roles in the assessment of teamwork. These two principles of cooperative learning may seem far apart and difficult to accomplish together, yet the success of team-based learning relies on the ability to design activities that balance both elements. Within group learning activities, there is a very fine line between collaboration and collusion

(Isaacs, 2002). Slavin (1995) describes the success of cooperative learning as the ability to have group goals but be capable of assessing individual accountability.

Peer and Self-Assessment

Peer and self-assessment methods have been widely used as variables to ensure that either or both individual accountability and positive interdependence have been achieved in team-based assessments. Learners have little experience with reflective assessment methods. They frequently have difficulty with evaluation and do not feel comfortable or confident in analyzing and criticizing their own and others' work. One useful strategy in teaching these skills is to begin with instructors' modeling and critiques. Once learners understand what is involved, and see examples, they are better able to engage in their own reflections and assessment of others (Yancey, 1998). It is important to scaffold the introduction of peer and self-assessment practices into a course.

Assessment of Learning

When learning becomes internalized, learners see their knowledge and skills developing from meaningful learning assignments. Externally, learners benefit from useful feedback that improves their learning performance and together improves the overall effectiveness of learning (Battersby, 1999). Authentic assessments support these goals at the course level, making sure that the students learn what the course intends for them to learn (facts, concepts, process, products, skills) and conducting assessment in a manner that is relevant, accurate, and valid. The following are supporting characteristics of an authentic assessment strategy.

- *Ongoing.* Many assessment points are included in the course and seamlessly integrated into the learning process to effectively assess the student's progress in different areas

- *Valid and reliable.* Using the right type of assessment method for what it is intended to assess

- *Comprehensive.* Should assess different skills, through different perspectives (instructors, students, other students)

- *Communicated.* Clearly defined task specifications, grading criteria, and feedback loops

- *Variety of methods.* Allowing for different techniques to evaluate the performance, gathering multiple sources of information

(Fenwick & Parsons, 2000)

It is important to note that as we consider the elements that constitute authentic assessment (e.g., ongoing and variety of methods), keep in mind some of the common challenges found in the implementation of team activities such as workload and the increased time that students spend managing team activities.

In order for a successful translation at the level of individual learning activity, it is key for assessment approaches to consider the following principles.

- Clearly link activities to learning objectives.

- Clearly establish the benchmarks of satisfactory performance before learner outcomes are measured.

- Clearly specify the task and the process (i.e., steps) students should follow to be successful.

- Provide clear and valuable feedback so that the assessment supports the learning process.

As we might expect, assessment provides data on learners' performance for grading purposes as well as information on the effectiveness of the instruction. Assessment and learning are intrinsically related, and the assessment methods and requirements probably have a greater influence on how and what learners learn than any other single factor (Boud, 1995b). Based on these principles we developed the Team Assessment Guidelines Checklist (TAGC) to be used to guide the development and evaluate the quality of the team assessments at the course and the activity level.

The TAGC can be used as a planning tool for development or as a quantitative measure of predetermined conditions. To facilitate the use and application of the guidelines we have developed a checklist (see Table 3.1) that contains all the elements that should be present in the design of team assessment. Despite criticisms and/or doubts expressed about the low validity and reliability of checklists, the use of checklists and criteria for evaluation is very common. There is a great demand for such instruments because of their ease of use and low cost. In addition, checklists help us remember important items and allocate merit to each relevant dimension. The checklist itself has no evaluative value, but in the right context it could be used as a guideline for the development of team activities (graded or not) and for diagnostic purposes. The tool allows the user to identify relationships concerning distinct instructional design items in the context of team assessment.

Table 3.1

Team Assessment Guidelines Checklist

Course-Level Team Assessment Strategy Checklist		
Element	**Present**	**Comments**
Instructional Design		
Match instructional objectives	☐ Yes ☐ No	
Match learner characteristics	☐ Yes ☐ No	
Match instructional strategies	☐ Yes ☐ No	
Assessment of Learning Ongoing	☐ Yes ☐ No	
Reliable and valid	☐ Yes ☐ No	
Comprehensive	☐ Yes ☐ No	
Communicated	☐ Yes ☐ No	
Variety of methods	☐ Yes ☐ No	

The TAGC consists of four general dimensions: instructional design, principles of cooperative learning, peer/self-evaluation, and assessment of learning (see Table 3.2). Each dimension consists of one or more items which help inform that dimension as described in the previous section. We will further examine the TAGC in the context of our case study.

CASE STUDY: COURSE DESIGN AND EVALUATION

Our case study provides a close look at the design and implementation of collaborative learning assessment methods within an interaction design course utilizing a mixed model of face-to-face and online learning. In harmony with program-level goals, the desired learning strategies and goals of

Table 3.2

Activity-Level Team Assessment Strategy Checklist

Element	Present	Comments
Instructional Design		
Match learning objective	☐ Yes ☐ No	
Process sequencing	☐ Yes ☐ No	
Principles of Cooperative Learning		
Individual accountability (at least one)		
• Self-evaluation	☐ Yes ☐ No	
• Peer evaluation	☐ Yes ☐ No	
• Individual contributions	☐ Yes ☐ No	
Positive interdependence (at least one)		
• Mutual goals (team assignments)	☐ Yes ☐ No	
• Team reward	☐ Yes ☐ No	
• Team process-defined roles	☐ Yes ☐ No	
• Shared resources	☐ Yes ☐ No	
Promoting interaction	☐ Yes ☐ No	
Team skills	☐ Yes ☐ No	
Group processing	☐ Yes ☐ No	
Peer/Self-Evaluation		
Modeled-scaffold	☐ Yes ☐ No	
Assessment of Learning		
Comprehensive	☐ Yes ☐ No	
Communicated		
• Assignment specifications are clear	☐ Yes ☐ No	
• Criteria for success is clearly stated	☐ Yes ☐ No	
• Type and time when feedback would be provided clearly stated	☐ Yes ☐ No	

the course include learning effectiveness, learner centeredness, responsiveness to workplace needs, and effective use of educational technology (Wakkary & Belfer, 2002).

The interaction design course is a third-year undergraduate course within an interactive arts program. Generally, the aims of the course are for the learners to understand what interaction design practice is and, within the practice, the need for design processes that are collaborative and human centered. The course adopts a studio-based approach to learning in order to simulate and provide hands-on experience with design activities and practice. Specific design processes the course investigates include collaboration, problem definition, awareness of the use of methods, iteration, development and use of prototypes, reflection, and communication of design processes and outcomes.

Course Design

The course consists of three five-week modules. The overall progress within the course begins in the first module with the introduction of the concepts of experience design and interaction design, and exploration of the processes of problem definition, that is, research and problem setting. The second module focuses on the introduction of the role of design methods and exploration of the processes of user-centered design methods and participatory design. The third module is a focus on further exploration of design methods, such as pattern language, but primarily aims to allow for a synthesis of concepts through application in longer-term group design projects.

Critical at this stage of the learner's understanding of design practice is the aim to establish three key principles and to allow these principles to be investigated through hands-on practice and experimentation. The first principle is that design is not solely in the control of designers, rather it requires the facilitation of co-designing with potential users. The second is that designers are not problem solvers, rather they are problem setters; that is, a key function of design is to continually engage and reengage in the process of setting the design problem, often from very abstract requirements. The third principle is that design is not about outcomes or artifacts, rather that designers create, modify, and innovate with design methods as much as, if not more than, outcomes. To the majority of students this represents a significant shift in their understanding of design, and therefore a practice-based learning environment is critical to the transformation required in their learning and understanding of these issues.

The course is designed to allow for the application of these principles in an iterative and practice-based process of problem setting, designing, and communication. In addition, the modules include discussion and reflection on conceptual content and design activity related to each team project. All of these activities are a mix of in-class, out-of-class, and online. The activities range to include the entire class, groups, or individuals (see Figure 3.1). The conceptual content and project descriptions are provided online in the learning management system. A sequenced set of learning activities iterate within each of the three modules. These activities include online presentations, key questions, play-types, assemblages, selected play-type reflection, assemblage postmortem, and assemblage reflection.

Online presentation. In each week for the first three weeks of the module, the course includes a presentation of concept-related resources in the form of readings, design examples, and online links. In addition, descriptions of class activities, assignments, and learning objectives are presented.

Key questions. Each week for the first three weeks of the module, learners post to the class discussion board a key question that relates to and cites two or more of the readings or examples from the online presentation. Learners engage in an online discussion based on the key questions before the scheduled class, and the key questions are discussed in class as part of the group reflection on the concepts within the online presentation. Key questions are an individual activity.

Play-type. Each week for the first three weeks of the module, teams ideate, plan, and make a design project referred to as a "play-type." The concept of the play-type is a very quick and experimental prototype. The instructed outcomes are purposely wide with few restrictions. Teams may choose to create a performance, video, poster, software, web site, product, artifact, conceptual idea, or audio work. The play-type must refer to or be a response to the concepts studied that week. The open-ended nature of the play-type assignment is readily identified as a greater challenge for the students. The play-types include a design brief, an in-class presentation, and the play-type itself. Play-types are a team activity.

Assemblage. Starting in the fourth week and presenting at the end of the module, teams produce an assemblage. An assemblage is a second iteration of one of the three play-types produced during the previous weeks.

Figure 3.1

Course Design Represented Using E²ML
(Botturi, 2003)

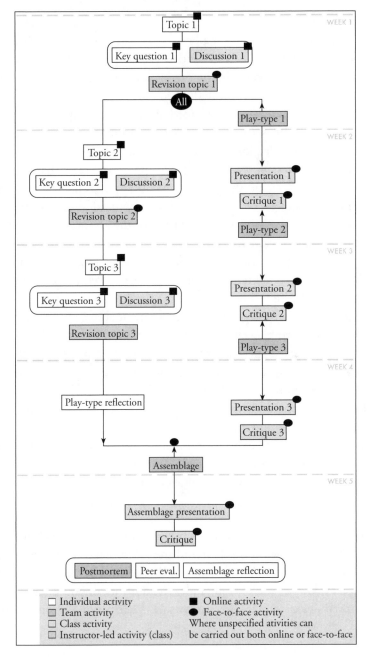

In addition to evolving the play-type further, the teams have an opportunity to respond to class and instructor critiques, as well as ideas from their individual reflections. The assemblages include a design brief, an in-class presentation, and the assemblage itself. Assemblages are a team activity.

Selected play-type reflection. During the fourth week of the module, learners select one of the three play-types their team has produced and complete a one-page reflection on that play-type. Learners are asked to address the following points in their reflection: provide a brief summary of the play-type; define their individual role within the team in producing the play-type; analyze the success (or failure) of the play-type from their perspective; describe what they have learned from doing the project. The selected play-type reflection is an individual activity.

Assemblage postmortem. The postmortem is a team-based written statement that reflects on the process, outcomes, objectives, team dynamics, and relative success of the project. It is submitted at the completion of the module, after the in-class presentation of the assemblage. Assemblage post-mortems are a team activity.

Assemblage reflection. Like the play-type reflection, learners are asked to submit an individual reflection on their team assemblage. Learners are asked to address the following points in their reflection: provide a brief summary of the assemblage; define their individual role within the team in producing the assemblage; describe the iteration of the assemblage from a play-type; analyze the success (or failure) of the assemblage from their perspective; describe what they have learned from doing the project. The assemblage reflection is an individual activity.

In modules one and two, teams are chosen using an automated tool provided by the learning managements system. The criteria used are grade point average, student's major or program stream, and gender. The goal is to create as diverse a team as possible. In the third module, the students choose their own teams. The typical team size is four to five students.

Evaluation

The course level evaluation assesses two key milestones of each module, a play-type selected by the student and the assemblage. The selected play-type is weighted at 25% of the overall grade while the assemblage is weighted at 35% of the overall grade. In addition, ongoing participation and contribution to class discussions in the form of key questions are weighted at 20%, and an equally strong weighting of 20% is given to peer evaluations.

Play-types and assemblages are evaluated in primarily the same fashion; however, further reflection and analysis of process is required of the assemblage assignment. The assignments have several artifacts that together form the overall assignment: a design brief, an in-class presentation, presentation documentation and support material (i.e., a physical prototype), individual reflection, and in the case of the assemblage, a team reflection or postmortem. The evaluation has an individual and a group component that are combined to give each student a grade for the play-type and assemblage.

The individual assessment primarily relies on the individual reflection and to some degree the student's performance during the in-class presentation. The criteria for individual assessment include:

Creative skills

- Level of engagement and focus in the process

- Overall energy devoted to the project

Reflection and presentation skills

- Ability to reflect and analyze one's own creative process and express it effectively in writing

- Ability to articulate the results and effects of one's own project outcome

    The instructions for the reflections ask for the following:

> Submit a one-page (10 pt, single-spaced) written reflection on one of the play-types your team completed this course. You choose which play-type you want to submit for assessment. The reflection should address these points: 1) brief summary of the play-type, 2) define your role in the play-type, 3) analyze the success (or failure) of the play-type from your perspective, 4) describe what you learned from doing the project. Please attach any links or supporting material you feel is necessary.

The assemblage reflection instructions are identical to the additional request of describing the iteration from the play-type to the assemblage.

The group component of the assessment relies on the design brief, the presentation, and support materials submitted. In the case of the assemblage, the group reflection or postmortem plays a key role in the evaluation of the assemblage. An overall grade is assigned based on all these artifacts. The criteria for group assessment includes:

Creative skills

- Aptitude for developing inventive and innovative strategies for identifying and solving the creative problem

- Willingness to experiment and to take a boundary-testing approach to the assignment

- Ability to visualize and translate an idea into an outcome

Technical skills and knowledge

- Ability to identify and adapt to the specific characteristics of the project

- Level of acquisition and application of technical skills and knowledge related to the project

- Demonstrated understanding and resolution of technical issues relating to the project

Reflection/presentation skills

- Ability to clearly express intentions and outcomes of the project

Each dimension is assessed on a scale of 50. Overall group activity assessment is out of 35, and the individual assessment is out of 15. Both scores are combined for an individual grade for a selected play-type or assemblage. Students receive separate written feedback and scores for the group and individual assessment. For example, if a group-submitted assemblage receives a grade of 28 out of 35, and the individual reflection receives a grade of 12 out of 15, the student's grade for the assemblage would be 40 out of 50. Another student from the same team with a lesser individual reflection score, for example, 9 out of 15, would receive a grade of 37 out of 50 for the assemblage. See Table 3.3 for an example of both group and individual feedback given by the instructor.

Table 3.3

Examples of Feedback to Students for Individual and Group Components

Example Feedback for Group Component

+ Problem setting was very good
+ Video interviews were well presented
+- Satisfactory communication and visualization of the idea through the video but the visualization of the prototype was weak
- Better analysis of the scope and dimension of the problem required
- Project would have benefited from clarification of the design situation, especially assessing all the users
+ Postmortem was strong and evidenced accurate reflection on the project's weaknesses and strengths

Score: 21/35

Example Feedback for Individual Component

+- Reasonable analysis and critical reflection—strong focus on the outcome but could have focused on the process as well
+ Strong engagement and role in the project is clear
- Writing and communication could be more effective—it was unclear at times, suffering from simple grammatical errors

Score: 12/15

At the end of each module, students complete peer evaluation forms for each of their team members. The assessment criteria is similar to the group assessment criteria with additional criteria related to team skills.

- *Participation and contribution.* Level of overall participation in and contribution to the team

- *Team communication skills.* Ability to communicate and listen effectively with other team members

- *Role.* Effectiveness as a team member in assuming roles that are complementary to the team

- *Leadership and innovation.* Demonstration of leadership and innovation that adds to the team's progress

- *Reliability.* Reliability as a team member in completing tasks

APPLYING THE GUIDELINES TO ASSESS THE QUALITY OF THE TEAM ASSESSMENT STRATEGY OF THIS COURSE

How does the TAGC help us to further diagnose and analyze our case study? We would like to test the tool of the TAGC, in hopes of making a diagnosis of the pedagogical soundness of the team assessments of the case study course. In addition we have provided some student comments as a result of institutional summative reviews of different deliveries of this course.

Course-Level Checklist Components

At the course level, the ordering of the content and the activities used to support the learning objectives is an important element of instructional design (Morrison, 2003). This course has effective ordering of content and processes (as shown earlier in Figure 3.1), which allows for an integrated flow of activities. The cohesiveness of the design carries across the five weeks of each module, and the team assessments integrate well within the overall learning context, addressing the learner characteristics and supporting the use of the present instructional strategies.

The assessment methods are clearly communicated and comprehensive enough to involve all participants of the course (see Table 3.4). The methods are also ongoing and diverse. For an outside evaluator there is a fine balance in maintaining efficacy and managing overload. Over the five-week module learners move back and forth between individual assessments through the key questions, to a team approach through the play-types and presentations, to a group approach through the critiques, coming back at the end of the module to an individual reflection and peer evaluation.

> I liked the fact that I know what to expect from class to class, and from module to module. There was enough structure to keep me up to date with the material and engaged, yet it wasn't overbearing.
>
> (IART317, fall 2002 student evaluations)

Activity-Level Checklist Components

At the activity level both team activities—the play-types and the assemblage—seem to be designed to take into consideration all instructional design, cooperative learning, peer/self-evaluation, and assessment of

Table 3.4

Checklist for Instructional Design and
Assessment Components: Overall Course

Element	Present	Comments
Instructional Design		
Match instructional objectives	✓ Yes	It is clearly stated in the learning objectives of the course that the learners would be designing and enacting collaborative processes.
Match learner characteristics	✓ Yes	The intended audience for the course is the third- and fourth-year learners that need to build their team skills to address the needs of the workforce.
Match instructional strategies	✓ Yes	It is clearly stated in the learning objectives of the course that the learners would be investigating and enacting collaborative processes.
Assessment of Learning		
Ongoing	✓ Yes	The course contains many assessment points (e.g., weekly key questions and play-type development/presentations).
Reliable and valid	✓ Yes	The assessment methods chosen are appropriate for the type of knowledge and skills assessed.
Comprehensive	✓ Yes	The course contains a comprehensive set of sources of information (e.g., student/selected play-type reflection, peer/peer evaluation, instructor/key question).
Communicated	✓ Yes	We have examples of the clear task specifications, grading criteria, and feedback provided.
Variety of methods	✓ Yes	The course contains a comprehensive set of assessment methods (e.g., selected play-type reflection, peer evaluation, team assemblage postmortem).

This is a checklist for instructional design and assessment components at the level of the overall course for our case study. The checklist looks for the presence of components and comments on details related to the specific course.

learning principles that we suggest for a good implementation of team assessment practices (see Table 3.5 and Table 3.6, respectively). For example, in the implementation of good cooperative learning practices, under the components of individual accountability and positive interdependence, more than one of the elements has been considered in the design. This creates a transparent process for students and addresses the issues that generate the greatest source of stress and challenges.

> I liked working on play-types and presenting them. It was fun and informative and helped give a kick in the butt to get working. It was also fun watching the progress of other teams, which also helped my team get some good ideas together. (IART316, fall 2002 student evaluation)

Table 3.5

Checklist for Instructional Design and Assessment Components: Play-Type Activity

Element	Present	Comments
Instructional Design		
Match learning objective	☐ Yes	Learners would be designing and enacting collaborative processes.
Process sequencing	☐ Yes	This activity is informed and informs other activities.
Principles of Cooperative Learning Individual accountability (at least one)		
• Self-evaluation	☐ Yes	Learners are required to submit a peer/self-evaluation, where they evaluate their contribution to the team.
• Peer evaluation	☐ Yes	Learners are required to submit a peer evaluation, where they evaluate their peers' contribution to the team.
• Individual contributions	☐ Yes	Learners are required to submit a selected play-type reflection, where they report their individual contributions and role as part of the team.

Positive interdependence
• Mutual goals
  (team assignments)   ☐ Yes   Learners need to work and
                                           present as a team.
• Team reward   X No
• Team process—defined roles   X No
• Shared resources   X No
Promoting interaction   ☐ Yes   Learners need to collaborate to put
                                           together an artifact and present.
Team skills   ☐ Yes   Learners are required to submit a peer
                                           evaluation, where they evaluate their
                                           own and their peers' team skills.
Group processing   X No

Peer/Self-Evaluation
Modeled-scaffold   ☐ Yes   Students are asked to reflect on their
                                           own contributions—selected play-type
                                           reflection—before submitting peer
                                           evaluations.

Assessment of Learning
Comprehensive   ☐ Yes   The activity contains a comprehensive
                                           set of sources of information
                                           (e.g., student/selected play-type
                                           reflection, peer/peer evaluation,
                                           instructor/critiques and selected
                                               play-type evaluation).
Communicated
• Assignment specifications   ☐ Yes   We have examples of the clear task
  are clear   specifications.
• Criteria for success is clearly ☐ Yes   We have examples of the clear grading
  stated   criteria.
• Type and time when feed-   ☐ Yes   Feedback is given after each team
  back would be provided   presentation through the critiques.
  clearly stated

This is a checklist for instructional design and assessment components at the activity level of our case study, specifically the play-type activity. The checklist looks for the presence of components and comments on details related to the specific course.

Table 3.6

Checklist for Instructional Design and Assessment Components:
Assemblage Activity

Element	Present	Comments
Instructional Design		
Match learning objective	☐ Yes	Learners would be designing and enacting collaborative processes.
Process sequencing	☐ Yes	This activity is informed and informs other activities.
Principles of Cooperative Learning		
Individual accountability (at least one)		
• Self-evaluation	☐ Yes	Learners are required to submit a peer/self-evaluation, where they evaluate their contribution to the team.
• Peer evaluation	☐ Yes	Learners are required to submit a peer evaluation, where they evaluate their peers' contribution to the team.
• Individual contributions	☐ Yes	Learners are required to submit an assemblage reflection, where they report their individual contributions and role as part of the team.
Positive interdependence		
• Mutual goals (team assignments)	☐ Yes	Learners need to work and present as a team.
• Team reward	X No	
• Team process—defined roles	X No	
• Shared resources	X No	
Promoting interaction	☐ Yes	Learners need to collaborate to put together an artifact and present.
Team skills	☐ Yes	Learners are required to submit a peer evaluation, where they evaluate their own and their peers' team skills.
Group processing	X No	
Peer/Self-Evaluation		
Modeled-scaffold	☐ Yes	Students are asked to reflect on their own contributions—assemblage reflection—before submitting peer evaluations.

Assessment of Learning

| Comprehensive | ☐ Yes | The activity contains a comprehensive set of sources of information (e.g., student/assemblage reflection, peer/peer evaluation, instructor/critique). |

Communicated
• Assignment specifications are clear	☐ Yes	We have examples of the clear task specifications.
• Criteria for success is clearly stated	☐ Yes	We have examples of the clear grading criteria.
• Type and time when feedback would be provided clearly stated.	☐ Yes	Feedback is given after the team presentation through the critique.

This is a checklist for instructional design and assessment components at the activity level of our case study, specifically the assemblage activity. The checklist looks for the presence of components and comments on details related to the specific course.

CONCLUSION

The design, development, and implementation of collaborative learning can become a very complicated task, especially if the learning activities are extended to the assessment of teamwork. Specifically, critical issues of team assessment need to be addressed to achieve effective learning, especially for the learners. Team assessment and activity are intrinsically interwoven into the instructional design process, but sometimes they are not given the required attention due to shortages in the areas of development time, understanding and experience of collaborative interventions, or understanding of the audience. The guidelines discussed can be used to support the overall goals for learning across programs and to support courses that utilize social constructivist approaches integrated with team assessment activities.

When courses are online, their organization and design often becomes more visible and easier to assess. Thus, the introduction of web-based educational technologies generates better conditions for the assessment of the instructional design. Good instructional design is a significant enabler of effective learning in a university context online and offline. It is a determining factor in the quality of online courses and student satisfaction.

This suggests there is significant advantage in the direct and formative evaluation of instructional design (Belfer & Nesbit, 2001).

The guidelines discussed can be used to influence instructional design practices. Equally, the guidelines checklist is a diagnostic tool for team assessment methods at any stage of the course development and delivery, that is, while the course is under development or at any point in the lifecycle of the course such as during delivery. Lastly, the guidelines encapsulate the challenges of team assessment and may prompt discussion in a course development team of the possibilities and challenges of designing collaborative learning activities.

Our aim has been to demonstrate the benefits of carrying out a specific diagnostic evaluation of the design of team activities and assessment within a course—easy to apply, time efficient, and effective.

4

Online Collaborative Assessment: Unpacking Process and Product

Bruce Burnett
Alan Roberts

The challenge for universities is not one of keeping pace with new technologies since they are often at the forefront of such developments. In contrast, the challenge is connected to pedagogy, and in particular, how the academy collectively comes to understand the framework of what it is to be an educated person in the 21st century. In short, this issue revolves around the question of how individuals should be equipped for knowledge-age work. Such work is epitomized by notions of virtual teams where innovative, collaborative team members located in differing global time zones use synchronous and asynchronous groupware technologies to pass the baton of conversation from one to another—a "hybrid that is both talking and writing yet isn't completely either" (Coate, 1997, p. 165). As the notion of the knowledge worker/learner takes hold in universities, assessment tasks within the institution are invariably moving from traditional print and face-to-face modes to those of a digital nature. This chapter argues that a corresponding digital realignment of assessment must extend to our thinking about both the assessment process and product.

This chapter describes assessment models developed in two Australian university undergraduate bachelor of education (BEd) units, where an overt attempt has been made to break from the prevailing paradigm of assessment tasks being merely transferred online. The thinking behind both models is significantly removed from traditional transmission, acquisition, and regurgitation patterns of learning and extends beyond simply a participation type learning activity. The focus of the assessment is on knowledge creation where throughout the process "an interplay between the growth of collective knowledge and of individual knowledge" (Bielaczyc & Collins, 1999, p. 276) is emphasized. Both models make extensive use of Bereiter's (2002) and Resnick's (2002) notion of employing technology as a tool to think with. This occurs to the extent that there is an active and creative approach to ideas rather than merely the act of transference. Significant to the discussion contained within the chapter is the belief that the conception of the task is as important to the assessment as the assessment is itself.

FIRST EXAMPLE

The first example relates to a cohort of pre-service business education teachers. These pre-service teachers were required to develop a guiding principles model that represented how they believed optimal learning experiences could be created for their own students. Working in groups of three and using a threaded discussion platform with the ability to attach files, participants downloaded and uploaded a Microsoft Word document, iteratively developing an increasingly sophisticated model. As this knowledge baton was passed between them, nothing more than the drawing features of Word to add boxes, labels, arrows, and color coding was required to create an ultimately sophisticated knowledge artifact—an assessable product. This interplay afforded an audit trail of student contributions made to the developing group model both in terms of the frequency of their contributions as well as the quality of their individual contributions. The use of small groups highlighted the contribution of individual student deliberations during the dialogue, allowing the individual's thinking and the level of contribution to be made explicit. Although the groups were composed of three individuals, all participants could view the model-building efforts of other groups in the cohort. Thus, there was a sense of Brown and Campione's (1994) "talk 'across groups' ... [to] provide comprehension checks on each other" (p. 235) as multiple simultaneous iterations occurred.

BACKGROUND TO EXAMPLE 1

Of the 42 pre-service business education teachers, 30 attended on-campus lectures, with the other 12 studying off campus through distance mode. These pre-service teachers range in age/experience from those completing an undergraduate BEd that includes a major in business education, to those who are already business graduates with many years of work experience and who are now completing the graduate entry BEd program. The unit of study related to this example, CLB 355 Accounting/Business Management Curriculum Studies 1, introduces these pre-service teachers to planning units of work and lesson plans. The major assignment is an authentic task requiring the pre-service teachers to develop units of work and lesson plans that they will use in their own teaching. A necessary part of the unit/lesson development process is that the pre-service teachers are introduced to the local educational authority's relevant syllabus document. However engaging, the syllabus document is rather technical in nature—some may say tedious. In the translating the syllabus document into units of work and lesson plans, we have been particularly concerned that the pre-service teachers keep uppermost in their minds a focus on achieving optimal learning experiences for their own students. Given that there is a major risk that the pre-service teachers will simply schedule the required content from the syllabus document to their planning, the notion of learning experiences has been introduced as the central design feature of the online assessment model.

UNPACKING ONLINE ASSESSMENT: EXAMPLE 1

Throughout the pre-service teachers' preparation there is a need that they explore various teaching and learning strategies; therefore, we model a collaborative knowledge-building activity through the use of information and communication technologies (ICT). Of particular importance is learning to work through this process with very limited resources, since the schools where these students will be employed have varying capacities in relation to technology. Thus, this approach does not require high levels of technical knowledge and uses essentially off-the-shelf software to achieve its goals of refocusing the pre-service teachers on notions of learning and demonstrating through participation—ICT mediated collaborative knowledge building.

The central tenets mentioned above are positioned as the precursors to the unit/lesson development tasks that the pre-service teachers are required to develop. This occurs via an online discussion forum in which the pre-service teachers are required to collaboratively develop the guiding principles model that represents how they believe optimal learning experiences could be created for their own students. This task of developing the guiding principles model was scaffolded to the extent that a set of leading questions was provided as a starting point and a requirement that the model be laid out in the form of a concept map. Questions included: In what ways could individual students learn? In what ways could groups learn? What is optimal learning? What appear to be the key elements of activities that promote optimal learning? An earlier exercise involving two minor tasks equipped the pre-service teachers with the limited technical skills necessary for this knowledge-building activity.

The pre-service teachers were assigned to groups of three, composed of one off-campus and two on-campus students. The threaded discussion platform used for the activity enabled files to be attached to the post, which is a common feature to many forums. While the forum itself contained many orientation statements and statements critiquing the developing model, the most significant work was evidenced in the attachments. A Microsoft Word document (limited to a single page) was repeatedly downloaded and uploaded by the group members, and with each iteration the guiding principles model (in the form of a concept map) reflected the increasing understanding of both the group and the individuals. A relatively sophisticated model was ultimately developed by each of the groups using nothing more than the drawing functions available within Word. Given the small group size (on reflection a group size of four may have been better) the contributions and nature of the contributions made by each group member is easily seen at each stage of development. The final group artifact—the guiding principles model—is an assessable product but also a valuable tool that the pre-service teachers will use as they develop their units of work and lesson plans. Figure 4.1 shows vignettes of one group, composed of Chris, Kia, and Brian. In Figure 4.1a Chris sketched out a possible starting point, and Kia picked up on the idea to provide the group with a very useful framework to further develop the model (Figure 4.1b). Brian used text boxes to add more detail to the model, and this approach was continued by Chris and Kia in subsequent iterations until the guiding principles model was complete (Figure 4.1c).

Figure 4.1
Vignettes of One Group's Development of Their Guiding Principles Model

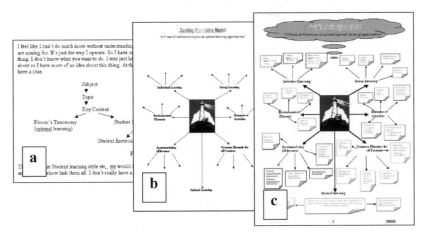

Although used for illustrative purposes with these pre-service teachers, the example here has considerable utility in higher education as an effective means to extend the threaded discussion forums beyond shallow forms of constructivism typically achieved via online discourse. The construction of the collaborative knowledge artifacts—on this occasion in the form of a concept map—affords a remarkable vehicle to synthesize the understandings from the individual to the collective group and from group-developed understandings back to the individual. It is in the development of the artifact that the interplay between individual and group knowledge introduced earlier is to be found.

ISSUES ENCOUNTERED IN EXAMPLE 1

It is evident, after implementation in 2002, that this approach supports the interplay between the members of each group and affords an audit trail of the contribution that each of the pre-service teacher education students makes to the model. This occurs both in terms of the frequency of their contributions as well as the quality of their individual contributions. Of particular interest is that the use of small groups highlights the contributions of individual student deliberations during the dialogue and model development. Hence, the individual's thinking and the level of contribution are made explicit to other members of the group and to the lecturer.

Another facet is that the asynchronous nature of the activity provides for the opportunity to reflect on the contributions of others—in short, to research and contribute as and when they were able. Given that the composition of the groups was a mix of on- and off-campus students, this approach afforded a digital bridge between the two modes of delivery. Feedback from formal evaluations conducted by the university indicates that this spinoff was interpreted as extremely positive by the off-campus students as it brought them into contact—albeit in an online format—and thus removed an inherent component of isolation common to this cohort of students. It is nonetheless clear that all students benefited through the exchange of ideas, since often the off-campus students are of a more mature age with a broader range of experiences that permeated throughout the combined knowledge-building exercise.

The use of concept maps have found favor in a number of contexts including business, public administration, and education (Lawless, Smee, & O'Shea, 1998). In focusing on their use in educational contexts, Lawson (as cited in Lawless, Smee, & O'Shea, 1998, p. 224) identified four functions of concept maps: 1) as instructional display (that is, of information), 2) as an evaluation device, 3) as a curriculum organizer, and 4) as an index for understanding. Feedback from the pre-service teachers confirms that the use of concept maps is an extremely useful framework to scaffold group responses. From an assessment standpoint, concept maps provide quantitative and qualitative measures of understanding.

In assessing the development of the guiding principles model it was possible in some measure to grade elements of process and product—the process being evidenced in the discussion forum archive and the resulting guiding principles model being the product. From the discussion forum archive, each individual's level of contribution is readily determined and only requires a tally of each individual's posts. In terms of the allocation of marks, however, the volume of contributions was only notionally rewarded (5 of the available 25 marks) as the quantity of posts by an individual did not necessarily equate with the worth or quality of the posts. For example, in several cases it was observed that individuals and groups engaged in social (nontask) discourse resulting in a higher number of posts to the forum, yet their model was no better for it. Quantifying the quality or significance of each individual's contribution to the total task is difficult and time-consuming; nonetheless, 5 of the 25 marks were awarded to this area. We acknowledge that larger cohorts could make this level of assessment rather onerous; indeed, we acknowledge that better measures and procedures do need to be developed in this regard (some of these are introduced in the second example within this chapter). Assessing the groups' final guiding principles model against established criteria was, by contrast, an easier task. Here the remaining 15 marks were allocated against the criteria of:

- Completeness—in terms of the group addressing the initial leading questions

- The perceived utility of the model as a guide to their subsequent unit and lesson planning

- The extent to which the model was supported by research

In summarizing this section the most significant aspect of this activity is the innovative integration of the relatively simple components of a threaded discussion forum: the features of Microsoft Word and notions of concept mapping as a means to facilitate a very successful and authentic collaborative knowledge-building activity, and the ability to assess the understanding of these pre-service teachers. Specifically, this first model has been successful in:

- Allowing for sophisticated knowledge building without the use of propriety software

- Engaging the participants in an authentic activity

- Simulating emergent, knowledge-age work practices in the ilk of the virtual team, resulting in enhanced learning opportunities for participants and the opportunity to assess both process and product

SECOND EXAMPLE

The second example—related to a multidisciplinary cohort of pre-service high-school education teachers—similarly capitalized on the interplay between developing individual and collective knowledge in relation to the use of ICTs in their own pedagogy. In this large unit (more than 750 students) multiple tutorials were conducted with each tutorial composed of approximately 28 students. In each tutorial, students were allocated to one of four seminar groups which then focused on one of four allocated topics related to technology and education: 1) access and equity, 2) technophobia and interfacing with the machine, 3) digital communication and publishing, and 4) language and the virtual classroom. Each group was required to explore their issue collectively while individuals choose a particular aspect of the topic to explore in depth. Following the model of jigsaw or peer tutoring, each group was required to conduct an in-depth ICT enhanced seminar on their topic that was aimed at facilitating understanding across the rest of the tutorial group. Additionally, the students had to develop individual components of a corporate or group web site focusing on their selected topic. Each individual site explored in considerable depth a single aspect of the topic while at the same time provided links to the other group members' pages. What was achieved was both an individual and group knowledge artifact that could be interpreted as a collaborative achievement.

BACKGROUND TO EXAMPLE 2

The following section outlines an approach to online assessment used by a large teacher education unit, CLB341 Language Technology and Education, with more than 750 students enrolled. Within the Australian context this unit is termed a foundation or compulsory unit that is undertaken by all secondary or high-school teacher-education students within their BEd. Over the six years the unit has been running, the assessment has changed in focus and evolved markedly as a result of our explicit desire to mold traditional participatory learning frameworks into an online format that focused on and aided knowledge creation at the group/collective and individual levels.

Principal subject matter within the unit relates to language, new literacies, and the manner in which new technologies and ICTs are interwoven into the contemporary educational matrix in high schools. At the core of the unit is the notion that a contemporary sociocultural understanding of language and technology helps educators shed light on the degree and manner in which new technologies have cemented particular positions and practices of pedagogy within schools. Hence, the unit is more concerned with the implications of technology to pedagogy than the actual technologies per se. Nonetheless, a critical component to the success of the unit is contingent upon minimum degrees of student competence in manipulating the various technologies under analysis. Content within the unit is heavily weighted toward 1) technology as a social activity that evolves and changes over time, and 2) the educational implications of the interconnections between technology, power, and discourse within the context of applied high school educational settings. This unit is co-taught across two schools or sections of the faculty: the School of Cultural and Language Studies in Education and the School of Mathematics, Science, and Technology Education.

THE INITIAL ONLINE ASSESSMENT PRODUCT

In the late 1990s the outward appearance of the unit stood as one taught over a standard 13-week semester with the nucleus consisting of a series of one-hour weekly theoretical-based lectures that unpacked the sociocultural dimensions of technology in educational settings. Lectures were followed each week by a 90-minute tutorial and a further 90-minute workshop in a computer laboratory. Class sizes were restricted to 28 students as there were a limited number of computers in the laboratories and students were required, in workshops, to perform a series of independent activities related to their assessment.

When the unit was first offered in the late 1990s, the multiliteracy skills of students ranged from first-time computer users to some students who were in many ways more competent at manipulating the technologies than their lecturers. An essential component in the early stages of the unit entailed developing teaching and resource strategies that targeted raising the multiliteracy skills of students so that they would be able to complete the practical components of assessment. Our approach was to offer a series of introductory computer-skills workshops at various times outside allotted tutorial/class times. Importantly, these optional skills-based workshops—covering the core skills of email, web searching, file management, and word processing—were accessed by approximately 20% to 30% of the student cohort. As secondary BEd students, each student specialized in two discipline areas such as English/history or biology/mathematics, and it was within this context that they were required to design and develop a basic web page that served as a platform for the presentation of an online learning resource or web quest-like activity. In addition to the web page, students also had to demonstrate competence in as series of basic/generic skills such as word processing and manipulation of graphics. The applied web site, in the shape of a web quest, served as the conduit through which students demonstrated such competence. For some students the skills obtained in the earlier workshops and tutorials became critical for the successful completion of this initial assessment item.

The initial assessment item consisted of an individual project where the students developed a simple three-page web site/web quest in computer workshops. This assessment item was discussed and analyzed in tutorial activities that preceded each workshop and was graded using the criteria listed in Table 4.1.

Table 4.1

Criteria Used to Provide Feedback for the Individual's Web Site

Design and Technical Aspects of Web Site	Fail	Poor	Satis-factory	Good	VG	Excellent
Functionality						
Basic principles of web design						
Aesthetic appeal						
Demonstrated competencies and skills in a range of generic programs used in the CLB341 workshop program						

Online Learning Activity	Fail	Poor	Satis-factory	Good	VG	Excellent
Critical reflection and engagement with the notion of online learning						
Considerations of language and technological implications for educational practice in the chosen curriculum area						
Organization						
Coherence						

Of note in this initial assessment paradigm was that although an overall quantitative or raw-score grade was allocated to the web site, we chose to assign qualitative values in terms of each of the criteria. Feedback from students indicated that they found the criteria useful in framing and structuring their web sites. In addition, students were expected to demonstrate a range of basic electronic/technology literacy skills through the application of a range of generic computer programs (i.e., word processing, spreadsheets, graphics programs, etc.) to specific educational contexts within their various discipline areas.

ISSUES ENCOUNTERED WITH THE INITIAL MODEL

On the basis of formal student evaluations conducted by the university, together with end-of-term staff-based evaluations, it became apparent that the initial assessment model succeeded in allowing students to reflect on the manner in which electronic technologies were affecting pedagogy in their chosen curriculum area. It was also evident that the initial assessment task allowed for the grounding of somewhat abstract sociocultural theoretical concepts of technology and pedagogy in a curriculum framework that was relevant and applied. Additionally, the assessment succeeded in focusing the students' attention on key aspects of their own technological literacy and helped raise these skills across large sections of the cohort. Consequently, the initial online assessment item succeeded in the three broad areas.

• Served as a skills-based learning activity for students lacking key techno/multiliteracies

• Enhanced a theoretical appreciation of broader sociocultural implications of technology and pedagogy

• Unpacked the potential of technology to enhance teaching and learning

Over an extremely short period of time, however, there emerged problems in each of these key areas. First, we found that the techno-literacy skills students were bringing to the unit changed dramatically. For example, over a three-year period the attendance at the basic computer skills workshops had dropped off to such an extent that the workshops were no longer the core component of the start of each semester/term. Consequently, the focus of the workshops became more aligned to providing a component of equity. Although optional workshops are still offered, we found that it is now possible to operate these skill-based sessions over the first two weeks of each semester. With initial help from the tutor/lecturer, it is now possible for students to work independently on a number of skill-based activities online via a dedicated web site, which students access as needed throughout the semester. Although we are still strongly committed to offering this service on equity grounds alone, evidence in the form of hits on this skills-based site in 2003 indicates that an ever decreasing number of students currently need such techno/multiliteracy core skills training.

Second, over the relatively short period from 2000 to 2002 we found that what students and teachers were interpreting as functional educational web sites had shifted markedly and that our initial online assessment item lacked any true relevance to real-life classrooms. Where in 1999 a simple website may have served as a workable online learning environment, by 2002 this same site was beginning to be described by students as both simplistic and pedagogically inappropriate.

The third area of transformation occurred as a result of our growing appreciation of the dynamics of online group work and our desire to begin to embed an overarching assessment schema that took into account concepts of the post-industrial worker and the information-rich learner. Of particular importance here was that we attempted not to limit our understandings of ICTs and online assessment to the electronic submission and marking of assignments. The substituting of digital copy for hardcopy, while perhaps administratively appealing (particularly with the advent of marking software), fails to capitalize on the learning opportunities afforded by technology. What we wanted to attempt was to build on a process/capacity to move and share individual and group generated digital copy via ICTs. In addition to instilling useful technical skills, we also felt that this component would begin to equip students for perceived emergent, knowledge-age practices necessitating collaborative effort, innovation, and knowledge building.

THE FINAL ONLINE ASSESSMENT FOR EXAMPLE 2

A major weakness with the initial design was that students were being asked to produce an online learning activity without any real in-depth understanding of web design and functionality. For this reason a major change has been putting in place strategies that better equip students with a more substantial understanding of the variables of online learning resources/environments. Despite this being an education-based unit in contrast to a creative arts–based unit, we felt that the most appropriate manner to achieve this goal would be to first require students to critically analyze the design and functionality of an existing online learning activity/web site potentially used within their secondary curriculum area. Hence, a minor piece of assessment required that students provide a critical academically structured discussion of a specific website/learning resource structured around a number of themes discussed in lectures. Using the design parameters outlined by Gallini (2001), a series of lectures addressed the key domains of background, design, and impact. The lectures were structured around a number of themes and issues such as the nature of an online resource versus an online learning activity, and how students would be able to locate such resources. Notions of design were also introduced in relation to issues of functionality, aesthetics, and language. In addition, students were introduced to notions of online pedagogy and, in particular, the components of desirable online learning.

A revised assessment format was implemented in 2002, with significant changes made to the online assessment artifact as both product and process. This new design begins with students allocated to small groups which are required to collectively investigate topics similar to those listed in the earlier design (i.e., access and equity, technophobia and interfacing with the machine, digital communication and publishing, and language and the virtual classroom). As individuals, students are also required to analyze and unpack the topic in more depth; this task makes up the major assessment piece which constitutes 60% of the student's final grade.

The task requires students to demonstrate skills in researching one of four critical issues listed above with the notion of jigsaw (Aronson, 1978) or peer tutoring (Brown & Campione, 1994) being central to the production of the final group and individual products. This begins with each group being required to conduct an in-depth ICT-enhanced seminar on their topic that is aimed at facilitating understanding across the rest of the tutorial group. This occurs before the students construct their web site and has been particularly successful in the synthesizing of critical reflections concerning the topic. These face-to-face seminars also serve as an opportunity for groups and individuals to workshop ideas and to discuss the major issues related to the topic in a nonthreatening setting with other groups within the tutorial. Although a compulsory component of the assessment, the seminar does not represent a significant factor in the students' final grades. After the seminar, students begin to develop their individual web site that serves as part of a larger group web site focusing on their selected topic. Individual sites explore, in substantial depth, explicit aspects of the topic while at the same time providing links to the other group members' pages.

Constraints on the structure of the online assessment item are relatively few, but it is essential that it be possible to navigate to and from a PowerPoint presentation that the group uses in the seminar, to and from each of the other group members' web sites, and to and from each student's individual academic essay response to the issue. In a similar manner to the initial assessment model discussed earlier, students are still required to display an awareness of, and generic skills in, using a number of electronic technologies/programs in educational settings.

What is achieved is both an individual and group knowledge artifact that can be interpreted as a collaborative achievement. Indeed, the use of the technology in this context is focused on facilitating student activity and is not concerned about pushing content on students and then testing it through online quizzes. This approach also extends beyond merely using a threaded discussion forum for discussing ideas—an approach that can at best provide for shallow constructivism. Rather, the students in these units actively develop a knowledge artifact as the cumulation of their combined efforts.

One of the major innovations has been a dedicated web site that lists the names of all students enrolled in the unit. Each name is linked to the actual web site being constructed by that student and provides not only an extremely useful aid for grading, but more importantly, a real-time inventory and register of the work of other students where ideas/knowledge are shared and distributed. Of note is that we have now moved to providing and using specific group and individual targeted criteria (see Table 4.2) that are applied holistically to the assessment piece as an aid to overall grading. These criteria also serve as feedback for students, which is an aspect that has been extremely well received.

Table 4.2

Criteria Used to Provide Feedback on the Group and Individual Web Site

Analysis of issues (group)	Academic conventions (individual)
Synthesis of issues (group)	Functional design of web site (individual)
Presentation (group)	Aesthetic design of web site (individual)
Selection of examples, illustrations or elaborations (individual)	Selection of language to suit genre of web publication (individual)
Understanding of issue (individual)	Clarity of expression and fluency of argument (individual)

Given the large number of students enrolled in the unit, the subsequent large number of tutorial groups, and a relatively large teaching team, we have been conscious of the need for consistency in how the criteria are applied to the grading process. To overcome this issue each of the criteria was clarified in much greater detail for the teaching team. A separate form was distributed across the teaching team describing each of the criteria and how that criteria was to be applied. This successfully added both rigor and consistency across the groups.

Many of the criteria themselves remained unchanged from the example discussed earlier. Importantly, we found that the key to applying such criteria consistently across the groups rested on the clarity and unambiguous nature of the descriptions as shown in Table 4.3 targeting functionality.

Table 4.3

**Expanded Criteria Used by the Teaching Team
to Enhance Consistency**

	Excellent	High	Satisfactory	Unsatisfactory
Functionality	Navigability is excellent with clearly and appropriately labeled links. Movement between pages is effective, evident, and logical, and achieved through comprehensible icons or text. All links work.	Navigability is achieved through clearly labeled links. Movement between pages is simple and effective and achieved through comprehensible icons or text. All links work.	Navigability is satisfactory with links generally clearly labeled. Movement between pages is achieved fairly simply through generally comprehensible icons or text. Most links work.	Navigability is poor. Links are not clearly labeled and/or movement between pages is difficult and/or inconsistent. Not all links work.

Overall, we found that providing expanded explanations for each of the criteria not only provided an aid for tutors to explain what was expected of students, but also dramatically improved consistency of grading across each of the groups. Hence, the assessment and grading process was explained in a series of targeted face-to-face lectures and in tutorials via the tangible analysis of existing web sites. It is our belief that this provided a much better scaffolding for the students to:

- Choose/design/construct an appropriate web site

- Critique critical aspects of design in their own and other students' sites

- Experiment with nonlinear modes of presenting their essays online

- Engage in collective forms of knowledge sharing/construction

CONCLUSION

In this chapter we discussed two different models of online assessment that provide insights into the imperatives associated with equipping individuals for the knowledge age. We believe that it is critical for educators to build into their online programs assessment items that target the students' capacity to innovate and collaboratively create knowledge with others. All higher education students, not just a specialized elite, need to work creatively with knowledge. As Drucker (1985) suggests, innovation needs to be the norm—simply part of the routine. The challenge for higher education, then, is how best to develop students who not only possess up-to-date knowledge but are able to participate in the creation of new knowledge as a normal part of their lives (Scardamalia & Bereiter, 2002). While assessment approaches will inevitably vary across higher education, educators need to be thinking quite differently about the processes and products of assessment. Indeed, we need to be mindful of the fact that how students learn depends in part on elements of pedagogy embedded in the assessment process. In this chapter, we provided two examples in which we made a deliberate effort to depart from the traditional thinking on how students learn. Central to this realignment has been an underpinning pedagogy that emphasizes knowledge creation through collaboratively constructed knowledge artifacts. While we look forward with anticipation to the new technologies that will be developed to support learning, the two examples in this chapter have focused on pedagogical innovation rather than technological innovation. Indeed, a significant strength of the approaches outlined in this chapter has been their demonstrated use of essentially off-the-shelf software that do not require high levels of technical knowledge or resources beyond those commonly found within most universities. We hope these examples will help others to position pedagogical innovation as the primary driver in higher education assessment and, in so doing, better position their students toward new knowledge-age practices.

NOTE

The authors would like to acknowledge the contribution of Dr. Margaret Lloyd to the assessment criteria listed in second model.

5

Using Virtual Learning Modules to Enhance and Assess Students' Critical Thinking and Writing Skills

David Hofmeister
Matt Thomas

Internet technology is revolutionizing the face and function of education at every level (Comeaux, 2002; Manzo, Manzo, & Estes, 2001) and affecting the teaching and learning processes available to students of every age (Thomas & Hofmeister, 2003). Whether the educational changes that technology provides to educators are made available to students depends on many factors. Perhaps the most important factor is the willingness of the teacher to develop technology-based lessons. The second most important factor is the availability of the technology for student learning. This curious reversal from the traditional notion that one needs to have technology before developing a technology-based learning activity is purposeful.

Currently, computer technology is available in schools, libraries, universities, and homes; Internet access is in place, and the road to integrating technology into learning is paved. Technology is here, and learning should include its sagacious use. In response to this reality, the authors of this chapter have been, and currently are, conducting research designed to examine the potential efficacy of merging traditional reading and writing activities with Internet discussion boards, forming what we have labeled Virtual Learning Circles, which we have worked with and written about for several years now (Hofmeister & Thomas, 2001; Thomas & Hofmeister, 2002a, 2002b, 2003).

In this chapter we first briefly revisit and update our view of the valuable impact that Internet technology, focused around well-planned use of online discussion boards and online text, can potentially have on learning. We then briefly describe our most current recommended structure for building Virtual Learning Modules (VLMs), and examine some sample student submissions from our in-process research. We follow these ideas with an updated discussion board assessment strategy and suggest other practical approaches for building scoring guides for assessing student discussion board work. We then, very briefly, discuss the potential need for a discussion board moderator and the skills he or she may need to further the online student discussions toward specific educational outcomes or goals. Our aim is to help instructors effectively build and use discussion board forums and to provide ideas for analyzing the resulting student thinking and writing. We hope this will facilitate active and optimal participation in online discussions, fostering true communities of learners.

THE PEDAGOGICAL VALUE OF ONLINE DISCUSSION BOARDS

As new Internet technology continues to enter our schools, we continue to believe that Internet discussion boards contain significant potential to increase the learning and development of participating students (c.f. Manzo, Manzo, & Albee, 2002; Thomas, 2001; Thomas & Hofmeister, 2002b, 2003). The growing research continues to be supportive of the medium's potential. For example, according to Bailey and Wright (2000), "the use of asynchronous learning via technologies, such as the Internet and discussion groups, provides an interactive methodology that can provide instruction comparable or superior to that offered in a traditional classroom" (pp. 4–5).

Clearly there are a number of theoretical advantages to the use of Internet discussion boards for instruction. In many respects, limitations posed to traditional educational settings in the areas of time, space, and place are removed, or at least alleviated, in the discussion board environment. The asynchronous nature of Internet discussion boards allows for messages to be posted and read later and responded to by other students, and provides potential for building extended threads or discussions involving multiple interactions. The opportunity to add information to the discussion is nearly

limitless as long as students have the time, access, and inclination to participate. When discussion boards are coordinated between schools, students
from different cultures, regions, religions, ages, perspectives, and with a range
of physical and mental strengths can work together on common topics. In so
doing, content subjects, along with individual student ideas and beliefs, can
enhance the learning interactions as students construct shared understandings of the material. Consequently, the discussion board interactions blend
instructional processes with students whose social and physical world is similar to and different from that of their potentially distant partners.

The flexibility of Internet discussion boards enables students to
manipulate information and facilitate communication through an interesting and varied instructional medium (Mioduser, Nachmias, Lahav, &
Oren, 2000). Variety comes through the discussion boards when they are
developed to foster writing interactions that stimulate different types of
responses and levels of cognition. For example, the use of reconstructive
and constructive discussion board prompts seems to elicit differing levels
of student writing complexity and cognitive complexity depending on the
type of prompt used. Interactions involving unique educational environments and diverse perspectives also seem to be a positive feature of discussion boards, as opportunities to invite diverse perspectives to any reading
and writing discussion are greatly increased.

Throughout our research and from our extensive use of discussion
boards in our own teaching, we have continued to observe that discussion
boards also seem to have these strengths:

- Utilization of the enduring nature of digital conversations (i.e., the
  conversation does not go away when class ends)

- The opportunity for common reading resources online (so that discussions can focus on a common topic without the need for everyone
  to have access to the same book or article)

- The potential for more precise grading of informal student interactions because the interactions are captured in print (and can then be
  evaluated as writing pieces)

- Increased student participation (in a regular classroom discussion,
  only a small percentage of the students usually participate, but in
  discussion board forums, all students can be expected to express
  their thoughts)

- An increased emphasis on student thoughts and reflections, rather than on personalities or interfering classroom social dynamics

The challenge, however, has been to fine-tune ways to structure, monitor, and assess usage of Internet discussion boards in order to yield optimal student growth. We continue to see that just using technology in the classroom is not necessarily at all like using it well or efficaciously. Therefore, what has been needed is carefully designed pedagogical plans or approaches that most effectively use Internet discussion boards for optimal student growth. This work has started taking place through the development, implementation, and refinement of Virtual Learning Circles (Hofmeister & Thomas, 2001; Thomas & Hofmeister, 2002a; 2002b; 2003). The VLMs that have been part of this research have been designed to facilitate effective use of Internet discussion boards when applied in a variety of subject areas at a variety of grade levels.

VIRTUAL LEARNING MODULES

VLMs are carefully organized activities located on electronic discussion boards that guide students through reading and reflective writing assignments with an expressed intent to engage others in digital conversation. These are ideal learning activities for courseware products such at Blackboard or WebCT because instructors are able to use web-based articles in association with questions to prompt student thought and interaction over the reading. The construction of the VLM online discussion board forums utilizes established reading, writing, and thinking pedagogy through a unique blending of aspects of reiterative reading (Crafton, 1983), Read-Encode-Annotate-Ponder ([REAP], Eanet & Manzo, 1976), About-Point (Martin, Lorton, Blanc, & Evans, 1977), and Literature Circles (Daniels, 1994). At this point in our research experiences, refining our earlier VLM construction plans, we now suggest that each VLM be carefully designed to include at least these eight key components:

- A common online text to read

- A reconstructive writing prompt that sends the reader back to the text so that specific elements are written about on the discussion board. For example: "This section is about _____ and the point is _____."

- A constructive writing prompt to promote text-tethered or beyond-the-lines thinking and writing about the text. For example: "The section that I read makes me think about..."

- An inquiry prompt. For example: "A question that I have about this is..."

- Directions to interact with fellow students by posting three replies (could include replies to replies as well)

- Gambits for adding a personal/human feel—addressing each person by name and signing each comment

- A brief explanation of the instructor's expectations for the student work

- Directions for the mechanical steps to be taken to complete the above tasks

See Figure 5.1 for a sample VLM that might be used in a college-level contemporary issues course.

In the next section of this chapter, on the topic of discussion board assessment, we will discuss some sample student work resulting from participation in Virtual Learning Module activities.

ASSESSMENT

Reflective Thinking and Cognitive Complexity

VLMs are organized to guide students through text reading and related responsive writings in order to interact with others about it. This process involves reflective thinking. Norman (1993) discusses reflective thinking as requiring deliberation. When one comes upon a certain condition, acts on it, and then thinks about what happened, reflective thought occurs as one makes inferences, determines implications, and remembers the experience and reflections. The following student reflections are illustrative of the results of encouraging this sort of student-to-student interaction in response to a common text/reading assignment (in this case, on the subject of increasing use of security cameras in public places). The sample student responses shown here are from middle school students in both suburban and rural schools located in the Midwest section of the United States (c.f. Thomas & Hofmeister, 2002b). While students knew one another

Figure 5.1
Sample Virtual Learning Module

Social Justice in Action: U2 and the Crises in Africa
VLC Sample Module: Seeking Social Justice—U2 singer's influence in politics of global humanitarian efforts.

1) Please read the following online link from the BBC regarding U2's activism for the cause of the AIDS crisis in Africa and the movement to forgive foreign debt in developing nations:
http://news.bbc.co.uk/1/hi/uk_politics/3047921.stm

2) Here on the discussion board forum, please write and post a response in which you answer these three writing prompts (please fill in the blanks with as much writing as you would like):
This section that I read is about _____ and the point is
_____.
This section that I read makes me think about _____.
A question that I have is _____.

3) Please post at least three reply comments to some of what your peers have written here on this discussion board forum. You may reply to the initial written responses or you may also reply to other replies, forming a sort of online conversation if you wish.
Please address the person you are responding to by name and sign your response. Please also be sure to write your responses carefully and thoroughly; your work will be assessed according to the scoring guide posted on the discussion board forum introduction page.

4) To begin posting your responses for steps 1–3 above, please click on the blue link above. Once there, to make your own initial comments, please click on "add new thread." To reply to your peers, please double-click on their responses and then click "reply" and post your reply accordingly. Please update the subject line to indicate the topic of your addition to the conversation.

---

within their respective eighth-grade classrooms, the use of pseudonyms on the discussion board reduced the knowledge of which person was interacting with whom.

In our research examples provided here, student responses to the questions asked were largely within what Norman suggests as reflective thought; the responses enabled students to combine existing knowledge and personal values about security cameras with new knowledge about security needs in a post–September 11, 2001, world. Within their reflections, we are able to read composites of significantly held beliefs relative to the topic. We also can analyze their thoughts vis-à-vis the information structures in the article and the students' personal thoughts and convictions through the presentation of their thinking on the discussion board. Although these don't include some of the VLM components (such as reconstructive responses or gambits) the following three-part thread presents three different students on the issue at hand.

> Subject: Security
> What about the good things these cameras could do? You would be safe when you went shopping. If you were robbed, mugged, or even beat up, they would catch the person because of the cameras.
>
> Subject: Re: Security
> That is true, there are many ways this could help. But there are also a lot of bad things you could do.
>
> Subject: Re: Security
> Although this is a benefit of having cameras, but at a great cost. Financially, it's not a cheap thing to assemble the command center and put cameras everywhere like they did. And as for being mugged and such in a city like Washington D.C. that's a problem they've created themselves. There they have strict laws about things you can carry to protect yourself, so your attacker may have a gun, but the law-abiding citizen would be without anything. I like the idea of simple solutions, before I have things that I value much more like privacy, invaded.

This rich dialogue among three middle school students clearly indicates new information and reflective thoughts on safety in various locations. However, the reader is left with ambiguity about the next part of the discussion, as discussants have dangled several weighty issues of perceived safety, counterbalanced with the likely loss of privacy. This exemplifies Norman's idea of reflective thinking, especially as personal values surfaced.

For another example, among the following four middle school students there is a range of contributions when juxtapositioned with the preceding three. These examples, from our research, are on the topic of using tax dollars to build a football stadium. The discussion was part of another

VLM, started just as the preceding example, with an online article to read and then two questions to consider:

Subject: Re: Football
Sports do rule but I'll have to disagree with building the new stadium because some people may not have the money to pay the taxes.

Subject: Re: Football
Yes I agree.

Subject: Re: Football
I totally agree with Duke. Some people may not have enough money.

Subject: Re: Football
I agree. Some people don't have the money to pay that much tax money.

As we read, the initial response set the dialogue for the remaining contributors. Unfortunately, the VLM did not include prohibitions against using "I agree" as a response to postings, so there is very limited information being developed by the additional three writers. As such, however, the two examples presented here establish a reasonable range of student posting and interaction on which to begin evaluating the student thinking produced by VLM participation.

In our VLM-specific research thus far, we have primarily focused on measuring the cognitive complexity of the student discussion board responses. Assessment of cognitive complexity of student discussion board responses is important in determining the effectiveness of VLMs. However, this sort of assessment initially proved somewhat difficult. There are limited measures of cognitive complexity available for rating written responses in traditional writing environments, and this challenge is magnified in VLMs where student written responses are rather like unique hybrids between short contributions to group conversations and traditional written responses. In order to help address this challenge, we developed, and have been refining, a simple cognitive complexity rating scale for use in the discussion board/VLM environment. It reflects the core dichotomy of the hierarchy of annotation types presented in the REAP reading, writing, and thinking strategy. See Figure 5.2 for the basic rating scale updated with hypothetical responses that might be found in a discussion board forum for a college service-learning course.

Figure 5.2

Cognitive Complexity Rating Scale With Sample Responses:
College-Level

Reconstructive Responses		Constructive Responses	
1	2	3	4
Simplistic Text-Dependent Response	Text-Dependent Response	Text-Independent Response	Text-Independent Response With Complexity
This article is about Habitat for Humanity. It is described as a program started nearly 30 years ago with the mission of building affordable housing in order to eliminate poverty housing and homelessness. The article talks about how the program works, who program affiliates are, how families are selected, who tends to contribute, and the effectiveness of the program.	This article is about the mission and history of Habitat for Humanity. Started nearly 30 years ago with the goal of building affordable housing to help eliminate poverty housing and homelessness, Habitat for Humanity, through local volunteer networks, has helped thousands of families toward home ownership. The article discusses the effectiveness of the program and the point is that it enables low-income families to make the transition from tenant to homeowner. The article points out that this is a significant outcome with positive social consequences.	This article is about Habitat for Humanity, a program designed to help provide affordable homeownership to low-income families. The article discusses the background and history of this program, and explains what a big difference homeownership can make in the lives and communities of those that Habitat has helped over the past 27 years. It seems to me that if the program has such positive social results, then it is certainly a worthwhile effort for all of those who get involved. Perhaps programs like this could help assist with other social problems as well. Maybe we should study what Habitat is doing more carefully and see what impact it is having on related social issues like crime, education, and unemployment.	This article is about Habitat for Humanity, a program designed to help provide affordable home ownership to low-income families. The article discusses the history of this program, and explains what a difference owning a home can make in the lives and communities of those that Habitat has helped. This reminds me of Rosanne Haggerty's program called "Common Ground." They too are trying to end homelessness and are taking on some creative projects that challenge some prevailing assumptions about homelessness. If programs like this have positive social results, then it is a worthwhile effort for all of those who get involved. Although I am sure there may be some other points of view to consider, perhaps our national agenda should highlight these things more. Perhaps programs like this could help assist with other social problems as well. Should we study what Habitat and Common Ground are doing more carefully and see what impact they are having on related social issues like crime, education, and unemployment? Perhaps the results will provoke a long overdue renaissance of conscience. I am going to search the Internet to see if I can learn more about the effectiveness of Habitat and Common Ground and see how policy makers are considering these findings.

The instrument develops along a four-part holistic continuum, which coincides with reconstructive and constructive prompts initiating the discussion. Our ongoing work with discussion board responses has led us to currently characterize the different point-values as follows.

Level 1. When the response reflects what was read with little to no extension of the information, the response is scored as a one. Responses at this level typically only summarize what the reading selection was about by reconstructing the basics of the author's message.

Level 2. Student reconstructive responses that extend slightly beyond basic summarizing of the reading receive a score of two. Responses at this level typically summarize what the reading was about and include treatment of the main point or points of the reading, but the thinking/writing does not extend to ideas beyond the text's message.

Level 3. When students respond to the text with constructive insights that extend beyond the text, they receive a score of three. Level-3 responses often discuss what the reading is about, what the point of it is, and then extend beyond that to include an application-level of thinking, or generally addressing the beyond-the-lines question of "So what?" Often this involves the expression of personal feelings in response to the reading, and an inclusion of related new ideas or questions that are provoked as a result of the reading and the student's reflecting on its message.

Level 4. When students respond to the text with constructive insights that extend beyond the text, and then add additional indicators of complexity, their responses receive a score of four. Level-4 responses often discuss what the reading is about and what the point of it is; include application-levels of thinking, or addressing the beyond-the-lines questions; and often involve the expression of personal feelings and related new ideas or questions that are provoked as a result of the reading and the student's reflecting on its message. In addition to these items that are also characteristic of Level-3 responses, Level-4 responses include other indicators of complexity such as the inclusion of related beyond-the-text examples, the acknowledgement of possible alternative viewpoints, savvy question-asking and possible next steps, and ideas and/or plans in response to the original reading.

We have found this basic instrument to have good face value as a reasonable and practical research tool for scoring student discussion board responses (from third grade through college); it helps provide a quantifiable look at the thinking evidenced in the students' discussion board postings. Simply, it provides a look at the cognitive complexity of student responses to the initial discussion board prompts and student-to-student interactions. However, as an instrument that will allow an instructor who has engaged in moderating the discussion board, the tool may have shortcomings because it is not designed to specifically account for an outside moderator. Our future VLM research goals, however, are to add (and assess the impact of) the additional variable of a discussion board moderator. We expect that moderators, who have acquired tools to elicit critical and complex thoughts from participants, will enhance the VLM discussions by providing an avenue for the students to reach more text-independent, cognitively complex thoughts.

CONSTRUCTING SCORING GUIDES

Much of our VLM assessment thus far has involved holistic assessment of cognitive complexity. However, instructors may wish to evaluate VLM discussion board responses for a number of other factors as well. The development and use of scoring guides or rubrics to determine the qualitative or quantitative significance of student comments in a discussion board forum can assist with this. Several decisions need to be made to construct a scoring guide or rubric. The Schreyer Institute for Innovative Learning (2001) suggests the following seven-step approach:

- Define the assignment

- Determine the areas you want to assess

- Determine the type of rubric or scoring guide you should use

- Define the key components

- Establish standards for performance for each assessment component

- Develop a scoring scale

- Adjust the rubric or scoring guide as needed

In step one, the goal and objectives for the discussion are defined so students know the kind of content that is or is not to be included in the discussion. The second area in the development of a rubric is determining what to assess. As noted, VLM discussion board activities can be excellent venues to express thoughts through writing. Assessment should be noted in terms of the content of students' writing and thinking. In addition, assessing the frequency and the timeliness of the posts is important. Were the posts all made on the same day to several different students or were posts made over several days during the discussion? How the student participated with others is another key area to assess. Were opinions sought from others? Were the posts engaging, leading to more discussion, or did a particular post simply shut down the discussion? Thus, there are content and skill areas as well as participation factors to include in the rubric.

With this three-element framework sketched for the rubric (content, skills, and participation), the third step is deciding whether the scoring will be holistic or analytic. The cognitive complexity scoring rubric described earlier and used in our VLM research studies is holistic. That is, student writings fit into a range of thoughts associated with generally described expectations. Holistic rubrics are generally easier to construct, but they are less precise when trying to determine a score when a posting seems to fall between two categories, and often they provide less direct feedback on specific criteria. The second type of rubric, an analytic approach, more carefully describes the specific expectations for a student. An analytic rubric is tighter, with carefully defined parameters for the students to follow. For example, in the area of participation, the expectation in a holistic rubric might be that the student will simply be a productive participant during the discussion. Conversely, an analytic rubric might specify that a student will be expected to participate at least three times, on three different days during the week-long discussion. Using the "sort by" command on discussion boards (or its equivalent, depending on the courseware platform being used) makes this particular expectation relatively simple for the instructor to assess.

Steps four and five of the rubric construction process are very important so that students and the teacher are in agreement about the particulars to be scored in the discussion. Here the rubric details the key components such as participation, writing skills, thinking skills, and supporting others in the discussion. It is important for the instructor to define each area. For example, what is participation? What are the primary writing conventions for which the instructor will be looking? What is expected in relation to cognitive complexity? Then in steps five and six, the rubric is developed to clearly explain the areas to be scored across a continuum. What constitutes a high, medium, or low score? How are the different criteria weighted in relation to the total score? Making certain that the criteria are weighted in accord with the instructor's expressed goals for the discussion board forum is important. Last, the instructor should consider the need to adjust the rubric after is it used, making any modifications that will improve it for its next use. See Figure 5.3 for a skeleton of a discussion board scoring guide that could be used for VLM assessment and which may further clarify the points developed above.

Figure 5.3

Possible VLM Discussion Board Assessment Rubric

VLM Goals	VLM Objectives		VLM Timeline	
	Needs Improvement 1	Satis-factory 2	Good 3	Excellent 4
Thinking				
Text-dependent summary expression				
Text-tethered or beyond-the-lines expression				
Question asking				
Use of examples				
Acknowledgment of multiple perspectives or alternative viewpoints				
Expression of next-steps ideas in response to the reading				
Writing				
General mechanics (spelling and punctuation)				
Syntax and diction				
Sentence structure				
Transitions				
Participation				
Frequency of contributions				
Timing of contributions				
Responding to colleague's specific questions				
General provision of feedback to colleagues				
Use of gambits and subject-line updates				
Thinking Total _____/24				
Writing Total _____/16				
Participation Total_____/20				
TOTAL _____/60				

MODERATION OF DISCUSSION BOARDS

In several research projects we have allowed the discussions to go forward without moderators (Hofmeister & Thomas, 2001; Thomas & Hofmeister, 2002a, 2002b). In such cases, the use of reconstructive and constructive discussion board prompts seem to elicit differing levels of student writing complexity and cognitive complexity depending on the type of prompt (Thomas & Hofmeister, 2002a). However, when students do not engage the discussion at the level a teacher expects, or the discussion wanders from the central question to sidebars and then disappears altogether, what should a discussion leader or moderator know, and what actions should he or she take?

Collison, Elbaum, Haavind, and Tinker (2000) offer two broad critical thinking categories in which discussion board moderators can engage. They term these categories "sharpening the focus" and "deepening the dialog." Under the first category, they list the importance of identifying direction, sorting ideas for relevance, and focusing the discussion on key points. In the second category they list the importance of questioning, making connections, and honoring multiple perspectives. In Figure 5.4 we have created a concept map of our own that presents a modified arrangement of these ideas, and that includes connections with some of the VLM constructs presented earlier in this chapter.

Effective moderating necessitates engagement with the participants to keep them focused on the VLM content at hand. Although a well-constructed VLM would ideally start the discussion with good focus, at points where the VLM discussion is drifting, the moderator could pull out key thoughts provided by others and selectively place ideas back into the discussion. It may be that the discussion is wandering because participants have not fully differentiated the main ideas from the supporting information. The moderator's writing could encourage students to focus on patterns of organization, encourage the identification of assumptions, or further the discussion by asking for the main or central ideas in the text.

Moderators also could help the VLM conversation move to higher levels of thinking. As the moderator encouraged participants to dig deeper, questions and responses would move beyond basic text-dependent summaries and instead elicit complex questions, text-tethered or text-independent connections, and interactions that invite and consider multiple perspectives.

Figure 5.4

Critical Thinking Constructs for Discussion Board Moderators

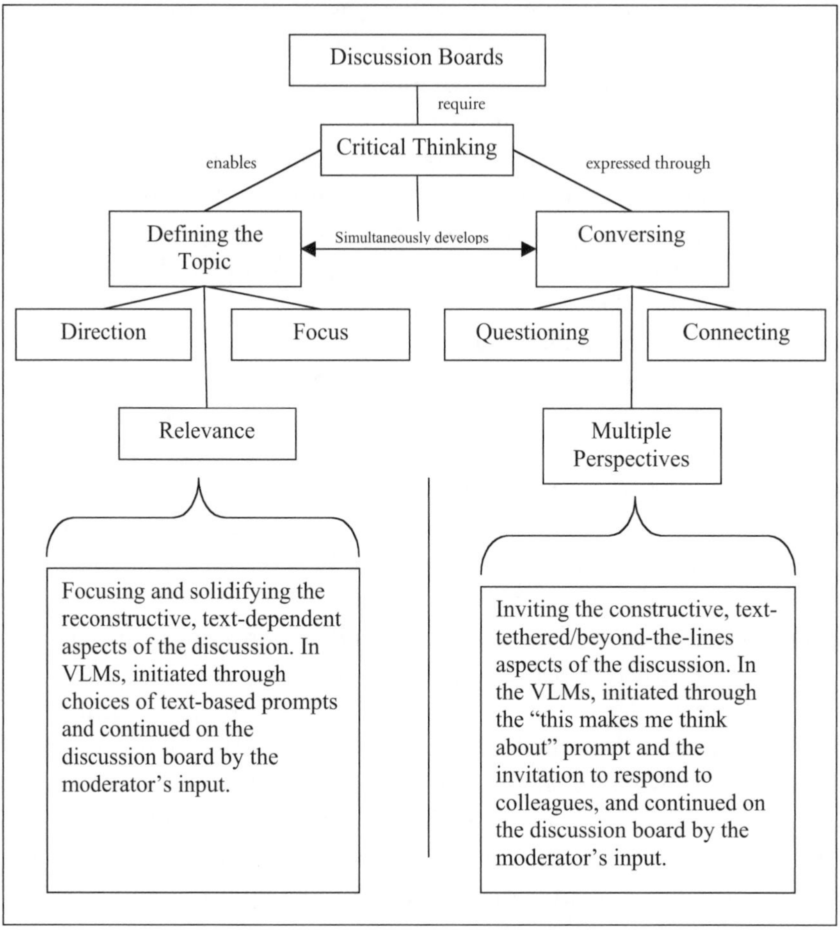

REFLECTIONS AND CONCLUSION

We feel that combining the VLM development and assessment components described earlier in this chapter with a moderator who remains
focused on the goal of the discussion and nudges students in that direction
while allowing students to push the discussion into the development of
new knowledge has the potential to propel the VLM discussion board
interactions to reach new levels of rich, thoughtful exchanges. As we look
to the future and plan for new VLM-with-moderators research, we are also

considering how we might best assess these sorts of VLM upgrades. We feel that we have found a complementary line of inquiry being investigated by Cole, Slocum, and Towns (2003) and Slocum, Towns, and Zielinksi (in press). They have developed a technique for mapping all the threads of a given discussion board forum, showing how certain postings spawn (or do not spawn) additional discussion (and how much additional discussion resulted). As such, this tool allows for a systematic identification of, presumably, the most fertile or thought-provoking postings. Our next-steps VLM goal then, is to combine our VLM structure and assessment ideas, including VLM-with-moderator activities, with this sort of mapping approach. We anticipate that this will allow us to identify, quantify, and characterize optimal moderator and student postings, which in turn, should allow us to continue to better understand how instructors can gain optimal educational benefit from Internet discussion boards. We certainly invite others to join us in this endeavor.

6

Developing and Implementing a Model for Assessing Collaborative E-Learning Processes and Products

Marianna Sigala

If you want to change student learning then change the methods of assessment.

—Cross, 1998, p. 120

E-learning environments enable students to engage with tutors and peers in ways that previously may have been impossible. Although e-learning is widely being adopted for enhancing and complementing tourism and hospitality instruction (Sigala & Christou, 2003), and its advantages for tourism and hospitality education are extensively argued (Cho, Schmelzer & McMahon, 2002; Sigala, 2002a; Williams & McKercher, 2001), little is known regarding the types of interaction by which students create new knowledge in e-learning. Pedagogical theories used for e-learning assume that interaction is important for successful courses, yet questions still exist regarding the nature and extent of online interactions and their effects on students' performance and learning processes. Indeed, past studies assessing e-learning platforms and benefits have mainly focused on examining students' perceptions and beliefs (Curtis & Lawson, 2001; Sigala, 2002b), and so, they have added little understanding and knowledge of how online learning occurs and how tutors can foster and support online learning processes. Moreover, because assessment plays a major role in driving student learning appropriately, the need to develop and implement robust assessment methods for assessing and supporting learning in virtual learning environments becomes indisputable.

This chapter contributes to the theoretical and practical implementation of e-learning by developing a model for evaluating students' participation in collaborative virtual learning environments. The tool that I used and implemented for assessing online collaborative learning was based on Gunawardena, Lowe, and Anderson's (1997) model initially developed for analyzing the content of discussion transcripts. I describe the practical implications of the model for assessing student learning by examining the model's application to online student debate developed to enhance classroom-based instruction. In addition, I illustrate and analyze how an alignment of the e-assessment strategies with the e-learning pedagogical strategies worked to foster and support the online learning processes.

METHODS AND MODELS FOR ASSESSING E-LEARNING AIMS

Constructivism argues that knowledge is created by searching for complexity and ambiguity, looking for and making connections among aspects of a situation and speculation. In this vein, e-learning activities enhance learning processes when they provide students with tools to think critically, analyze situations, search for evidence, and seek links between a specific situation and their prior knowledge and experience. Collaboration also aims to create analytical and critical learning competencies through social (interpersonal) processes by which a small group of students work together to complete a task designed to promote learning. This interactive approach enhances learning by allowing individuals to exercise, verify, solidify, and improve their mental models. The learner actively constructs knowledge by formulating ideas into words, and these ideas are built upon through reactions and responses of peers. In other words, individual learning is a result of group processes; learning is not only active but interactive. Collaboration is also seen as a variation of constructivism that stresses the cooperative efforts among students and instructors.

However, e-learning activities and processes are not complete and may not lead to the desirable learning outcomes unless they are integrated and aligned with appropriate assessment strategies. It is common that assessment-related tasks attract students' attention at the expense of non-assessed tasks. Thus, assessment criteria and processes can significantly direct, motivate, and guide students' learning processes. In this light, interest in the evaluation of e-learning and online discussion forums is continuously increasing and demonstrated in the great number of tools applied for teasing out key aspects of the interaction that can lead to improvements in online learning environments (Pitman, Gosper, & Rich, 1999). However, the appropriateness and impact of such tools on reliably assessing e-learning processes and outcomes as well as on fostering and supporting skills development are not always effective, nor do they support student-centered learning. In general, e-assessment methods are classified into two categories, namely, quantitative and qualitative assessment tools.

Quantitative methods aimed at assessing the amount, frequency, and direction/interaction of online discussions have pushed instructors to calculate statistics such as number of online users, frequency of access, number of messages per student, number of threads/messages per thread, or to develop message maps for reflecting the flow of communication within the group (Levin, Kim, & Riel, 1990). Although such metrics are good at identifying the level of students' adoption and engagement in e-learning processes, there is a danger of implying that the level of online participation reflects the level of learning (Mason, 1992). Moreover, such assessment metrics are limited in their ability to assess and motivate students toward skill development simply because they ignore message content. Instead, assessing students solely based on their level of online participation may lead to information/message overload that has nothing to do with the learning task; limited student guidance and direction as to what has to be achieved and how; and increased student stress when catching up on and reading messages leaves limited time for reading, reflection, concepts internalization, and assessment.

Qualitative assessment methods aim to address the limitations of previous metrics by exploiting the transparency of online discussions (i.e., the fact that all communication is easily organized, stored, and retrieved) and analyzing text-based archives/transcripts for understanding and evaluating e-learning processes. This is achieved by first breaking the transcript down into small units and then classifying these units according to the content. Different approaches have been developed and applied for identifying unit categories. Categories may be defined retrospectively, in order to capture the flavor of a particular forum (e.g., McLoughlin, 2002; Mowrer, 1996), or a priori, based on the learning processes and tasks in which theory implies that students should be engaged to enhance their learning. There are two reasons why the second level of analysis is needed to evaluate e-learning and guide the use of online discussion environments. First, students are assessed based on evidence of the learning processes that they have been engaged. Secondly, by making students aware of the assessment criteria (i.e., the predefined unit categories) in advance, instructors can acquaint students with the learning processes while also directing and motivating their efforts toward the tasks they need to engage.

A gestalt approach to analyzing the interaction of an entire online conference is central to Gunawardena et al.'s (1997) purpose in order to evaluate evidence for the social construction of knowledge, whereby learning is based on the shared construction of knowledge. Their preferred method of content analysis was developed to capture the progression of ideas as they were reflected at different phases of a forum discussion or debate.

- *Sharing/comparing information.* This phase may include an observation, opinion, agreement, corroborating example, clarification, and/or identification of a problem.

- *Discovery and exploration of dissonance or inconsistency among the ideas/concepts or statements advanced by other participants.* This is defined as an inconsistency between a new observation and the learners' existing knowledge and thinking skills (e.g. identification of differences of terms/concepts/schema and/or questions to clarify the extent of disagreement).

- *Negotiating meaning and co-construction of knowledge.* For example, negotiation/clarification of the meaning of terms, detection of areas of agreement, proposal of a compromise/co-construction.

- *Testing and modification of proposed synthesis.* Testing against an existing cognitive schema, personal experience, formal data experimentation, contradictory data from the literature.

- *Agreement, statements, and application of newly constructed meaning.* This includes summarizing agreements/meta-cognitive statements showing new knowledge construction and application.

Overall, it becomes evident that assessment of online collaborative learning should not focus solely on metrics reflecting the quantity of students' interaction but also on assessment criteria that consider the quality and learning ability of students' interactions. To that end, the following section demonstrates how Gunawardena et al.'s (1997) constructivist model of online assessment has been applied for designing collaborative e-assessment strategies and integrating them with e-learning strategies that can motivate and foster the development of students' learning processes and outcomes.

DEVELOPING ONLINE LEARNING STRATEGIES: AIMS AND ACTIVITIES

The virtual learning environment was developed in order to support and enhance traditional classroom-based instruction and learning. Specifically, online forums were developed to enhance the classroom-based teaching of a third-year module, Information and Communication Technologies (ICT) in Tourism and Hospitality, attended by 151 students. Online forums were created to allow students to exchange ideas among themselves and with the lecturer asynchronously (through email) and synchronously (e.g., chat room sessions) and create a data center to store, update, and access teaching and learning material of the modules in a secure environment (lecture notes/presentations, working papers/reports, bookmarks).

The Yahoo! service (http://groups.yahoo.com/) was used for creating online forums (see Figure 6.1) that had:

- *A message area.* Group members can receive/send emails and send and access/retrieve any message sent to the group by using the web mail

- *File area.* An area whereby teaching and learning material can be stored, accessed, and downloaded by any group member (a directory structure was developed to make navigation and searching easier)

- *Bookmark area.* Bookmarks of relevant material, e-journals, associations, research centers, and so on were stored in a specific location because that was the area that was updated more regularly

- *Other features,* including chat sessions, polls, members' area (profile, interests), and a calendar

Yahoo! groups were used because of their familiarity and popularity among students as well as previous evidence of their good performance in e-learning (Joia, 2002). Yahoo! groups were also easy to develop and implement in a very short time and did not require any expertise in software and web site design, and the latter was also familiar and easy to use by students.

Figure 6.1

Yahoo! Groups Web Site Interface and E-Learning Tools

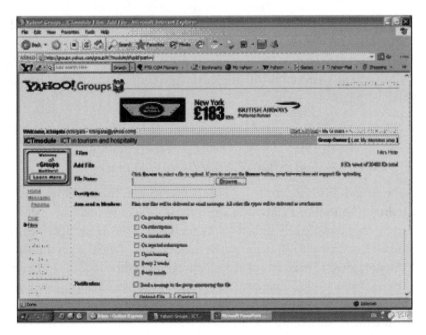

The online forum involved the accomplishment of a group task (Salmon, 2002) that aimed at enhancing students' critical, analytical, communication, and meta-cognitive skills. Specifically, the online task required students to form groups and participate in an online community in which pairs of groups would debate contrasting arguments. The forums were monitored and moderated on a weekly basis by the students, through discussion summary reports, and the lecturer, through formative feedback. The detailed process of the task is explained in Table 6.1. Thus, overall, in accomplishing the task, students had to develop and practice skills and qualities in searching and reading relevant information; internalizing knowledge and explaining it to others; listening/reading and understanding others' views/experiences; reflecting on, critically assessing, and identifying the relation/conflict among different views; and synthesizing, testing, negotiating, and agreeing on concepts for developing meta-cognitive knowledge. In other words, the online task was designed in a way that directed students to practice, engage in, and finally demonstrate evidence of all Gunawardena et al.'s (1997) online constructivism learning processes. Prior to asking students to exchange arguments online, a demonstration debate was initiated in the classroom in order to acquaint students with the processes and tasks they were expected to accomplish online. The classroom discussion provided explanations of the assignments and the assessment procedures for these assignments. Assessment was holistically linked with the learning strategies and as it is also explained below.

DEVELOPING AND ALIGNING ONLINE ASSESSMENT STRATEGIES WITH LEARNING GOALS

To foster and motivate students' engagement in online activities, while also directing them to elaborate appropriate learning processes, the e-learning task was directly linked to the module's assessment. Specifically, a holistic e-assessment strategy was developed and aligned with the aims of the previously analyzed learning strategy (see Table 6.2). Moreover, the e-assessment strategy gradually guided students into the development of cognitive skills, as it included assessment tasks that evaluated not only the quality of final learning outcomes/products (e.g., essay) but also the learning processes used for achieving the former. Analytically, student contributions to the learning processes were assessed in terms of student performance in isolated learning tasks (e.g., five individual messages) and student ability to use, reflect, assess, and exploit other contributions in the learning processes for accomplishing an outcome or developing future learning strategies. So, students' reading and internalization of knowledge, ability to express themselves on a topic, ability to engage, negotiate meaning, respond to other students' contributions, all while concentrating on their own line of thought, were evaluated through assessment 1 (see Table 6.2). Students' ability to synthesize and present arguments was evaluated through assessments 2 and 3. Assessment 3 also focused on evaluating students' meta-cognitive skills, while assessment 4 aimed at making students think about, reflect, and evaluate their individual and group learning strategies. In other words, assessment 4 was designed for enabling students to better learn how to learn while also illustrating how they could also possibly transfer and develop more effective learning strategies in other modules.

Table 6.1
E-Learning Strategy: Forum Learning Activities, Processes, and Tasks/Products

Module	Online Group Task
	Conduct a debate with affirmative and negative ideas, with the instructor as the facilitator.
	Group Task Guidelines and Requirements
	The tasks, concepts, and online forum were explained, introduced, and shown in classroom instruction. Nine weeks were available for online debate. One (different) student had to summarize online arguments every week and email a summary to the tutor and the group (in order to diagnose problems, facilitate/moderate discussions, provide formative assessment/feedback). Group summaries were uploaded in the file area of the group for online access. The weekly task for each group was to read and respond to the arguments made by the groups debating the opposite argument to theirs. One student had to write a final report summarizing the whole debate presented by his or her team and submit it to the tutor in week 10. The module assignment (submitted in week 12) was an essay that had a similar topic to the online debate. At any time, students could retrieve any message posted by any team member through the web mail. This allowed students to build and develop stronger arguments, exchange resources, etc.
ICT in tourism and hospitality (third-year, BA, 151 students, 15 Yahoo! groups)	Students were put into groups of 10 (approximately). Each group had to debate one of the following issues: • ICT applications have a negative impact on service quality in hotel guests-staff encounters. • ICT applications have a positive impact on service quality in hotel guests-staff encounters.

Table 6.2

E-Assessment Strategy: Aligning Assessment Tasks With Learning Outcomes and Processes

Assessment Task	Description of Assessment Task	Level of Learning Process Addressed	Allocated Marks
1 (learning process)	• Student submission and selection of his or her five best messages contributed to the online debate • Each message supported by another message to illustrate an ability to interact and build on other contributions	Identify and read, internalize, express, respond, and engage in debates, negotiate meaning	10%
2 (learning process)	• One summary of a weekly debate among two groups	Synthesize, contextualize	10%
3 (learning product and process)	• Individual essay on a topic directly related to the online discussion, for example, "Analyze how a five-star hotel operator can effectively exploit and implement ICT for enhancing the quality of the customer service provided" • Online messages are expected to be incorporated into the essay as evidence understanding online debates; quotations, comments, and assessment of other comments accounted for 5% of the essay mark	Assessment, synthesize, meta-cognitive skills	20%
4 (learning product)	Learning diary: reflection and assessment of group's and individuals' learning strategy and suggestions for future improvement	Reflect and assess on learning processes and development of learning strategies; learn how to learn, transferable skills	10%
5 (learning product)	Exam	Various skills	50%

It becomes evident that students are judged on both their individual and team contributions. Indeed, the aim was to achieve a good balance and interdependence between individual and team/community assessment tasks and marks in order to foster and support the development of the spirit and culture of an online virtual learning community. Indeed, students could not get marks by relying only on their own contributions, as the latter had to be supported by and related to interactions with other students. In other words, assignments were designed so that they would support the group coherence and cohesion, as students worked together and learned to rely on each other. In this way, these assignments were important and instrumental in developing the culture of the online learning community.

To promote student learning it is important to introduce a formative type of assessment for the purpose of providing feedback to students at interval times throughout their project. Thus assignment 2 was designed and implemented for this purpose. This type of interval feedback accomplishes several important functions of learning and instruction.

- Appraises and motivates good performance

- Guides students to the appropriate directions, while also avoiding disappointing results at the end of the module

- Enables students to catch up with online debates and exchange views among groups

- Helps students contextualize arguments

- Enhances students' synthesizing skills; facilitates students in writing their essays

- Helps the instructor in moderating online discussions (reading summaries, not all messages)

Previous findings (Mcdonald, 2003; Sigala, 2000b) have shown that students need time and practice if they are to become effective online collaborators. The reflective exercise (assignment 4) was devised in order to encourage students to reflect on and assess the process of online collaboration that was used and then produce a strategy for future collaboration. In this way, the exercise aimed at developing students' skills for online collaboration in an incremental way for subsequent years and modules. Indeed, in his e-assessment practices, Mcdonald (2003) reported that many students had found the forward planning very helpful as it was an opportunity to reflect on their experiences of online collaboration as well as a forum for discussing procedures and working practices. Finally, this reflective log was also useful for gathering students' feedback regarding the effectiveness of the e-learning platform and strategy as well as the good and bad practices. This feedback was found to be extremely useful in further designing, implementing, and improving e-learning strategies for the following years. (Some of the feedback and lessons learned are reported in Table 6.2, shown earlier.)

CONCLUSIONS

Although successful online instruction is assumed to be vitally dependent on student interactions, little knowledge exists regarding how to assess students' online interactions in order to motivate and foster online learning processes and knowledge construction. Moreover, the impact of students' interactions on their performance is unknown but critical for the implementation of e-assessment strategies. To fill this gap, this chapter demonstrated how Gunawardena et al.'s (1997) constructivist model of online assessment has been applied for designing collaborative e-assessment strategies and integrating/aligning them with e-learning strategies that can in turn motivate and foster the development of students' learning processes and outcomes.

Specifically, the case study reaffirmed the importance of assessment in underpinning e-learning pedagogy. Assessment should play a crucial role in helping students become effective online collaborators. More students participated in online collaborative activities when the latter were linked to assessment, while such assignments also had a positive effect on the quality and coverage of the online debate itself, as students were evaluated on the quality of the online discussions they were generating as a group and not as individuals. Thus, the case study illustrated how to foster and develop an online collaborative learning community culture. The case study also demonstrated how online collaborative activities and assessment can be used in an incremental way to support the gradual development of skills. Therefore, students should be assisted in becoming motivated, skilled, and active members of online communities so that they can contribute substantially to the learning processes.

7

Enriching Online Assessment Using Interactive Digital Video

Tony Hall
Conor Molan
Liam Bannon
Eamonn Murphy

The role of information and communication technologies (ICT) in education, and in particular, higher or third-level education, has become a contentious issue. In third-level education, very substantial amounts of money (estimated at $2.7 billion in the U.S. for the academic year 1999–2000, for higher education alone [Cuban, 2001]) have been invested in equipping lecture halls and campuses with the latest in broadband and Internet access technologies. The rationale is that these technologies will help lecturers and third-level teaching staff to better cope with large class numbers and provide a more student-centered alternative to traditional "chalk and talk" lecturing (Bates, 2002; Laurillard, 1993). The rationale is also that students, because they can access course content whenever they need to over the web, will be able to pace their learning as best suits them (Bates, 2002). However, a number of authors are pointedly more pessimistic about the role of ICT in education. Concerning computing in higher education, Noble (1999; 2002) describes ICT as "a technological tape worm in the guts of higher education" (1999, ¶ 45) which, he argues, is being used as an inexpensive proxy for instruction by lecturers and tutors. McGovern (2002) contends that "If learning is learning with people, then elearning is learning with content. It is the very removal of people . . . that has attracted many businesses to the Web.

Remove people, the thinking goes, and you remove costs" (¶ 4). Furthermore, Stevens (2002) has argued that "This has become an era of intense
efforts around standards, accountability, and socially consequential tests
for the masses. It has become an era of aspiring technology millionaires
for whom education is an enormous open market. In short, it has become
an era of Big education" (pp. 269–270).

COURSE DESCRIPTION AND EVALUATION GOALS

The emergence in recent years of blended learning is creating new
potential to transcend problematic, substitutive notions of ICT in education and create new possibilities for instruction and learning, where
effective aspects of conventional or traditional pedagogy are synergisti-
cally combined with the potential of new instructional artifacts and
tools like the web (Laurillard, 2003). The course we evaluated and
helped to redesign is a blended mathematics and statistics course, course
code MA4704, normally undertaken by approximately 200 (197 students in the spring semester of 2002) computer science, engineering,
and applied mathematics students in the spring semester each academic
year at the University of Limerick, Ireland. The new blended course
comprises tutorials, an interactive web site, rapid response email support, and additional weekly help sessions in the University of Limerick
Mathematics Learning Centre. The intention of the course design team
was to create an effective and synergistic combination of face-to-face
instruction and novel technologies and instructional tools. The motivation in designing the course was to conserve what works well currently,
in lectures, tutorials, and study groups, and augment this with innovative web-based instruction. The overall rationale for the new course was
to endeavor to motivate and encourage "more able" students, and to
reduce course attrition/failure rates by providing "weaker" students with
substantive web-based ancillary support.

A multidisciplinary team developed the interactive instructional web
site (available at http://www.ul.ie/~e-stats) for the new course. The team
members came from a range of backgrounds, including graphic design,
biology, multimedia, computing, science teaching, and computer-based
training. The team was composed of an instructional designer, two
graphic designers, a software engineer, a web specialist, a project manager,
a content quality assurance lead, one teaching assistant, one tutor, and

the lecturer. The web site for the new course took approximately nine months to design and implement. Our role was to evaluate the course, both its offline and online aspects, and to help to redesign and further develop the course according to the findings of our evaluation.

Addressing multiple variables and trying to understand and appraise the complex interplay of students' offline and online interactions were perhaps the most significant challenges we faced as evaluators of the novel course.

Our remit was to provide third-party, objective assessment of the course, and generate ideas to direct and inform the further development and improvement of the course. However, our role was made more complex by the many facets we had to examine in order to create a comprehensive picture of students' involvement in the course, and whether the course was, in effect, enhancing students' learning of statistics. In order to help tease apart the different concerns and prioritize the salient issues, the first part of our evaluation process involved identifying specifically what our main analytic concerns would be. We determined to focus on 1) assessing the instructional effectiveness and usability of the course tool, the interactive web site, and 2) ascertaining some sense of the overall pedagogical efficacy of the novel course. And, considering that the latter entailed examining a number of different aspects of the course, we determined that no one heuristic or evaluative technique would be sufficient. Therefore, since we were concerned with a set of different features, we determined that a combination of evaluation techniques would be required to effectively appraise the different facets of the new course, which we identified as an important focus.

EVALUATION OF INSTRUCTIONAL DESIGN

We applied the Thinking Aloud (TA) evaluation protocol in assessing the usability of the web site. For this part of the evaluation, we asked three students to follow the protocol as they completed a new topic on the web site. In our computer lab, we observed the students interacting individually with the course web site, and we also asked that the students enunciate their thoughts. We asked students to orally report their thoughts and explain their actions as they clicked their way through the site. We also asked students if they would try to explain what learning goals they were trying to achieve as they used the web site. We recorded the sessions on

Assessing Online Learning

digital video, and these proved a valuable record of user-testing post-ex-facto. We found the digital video record very useful for retrospective analysis and discussion.

This application of the TA protocol helped us to identify usability problems with the web site. Additionally, by asking the students to explain the learning objectives they were trying to achieve in using specific parts of the web site, we were able to clarify some of the benefits of the web site as an aid to student learning. We also identified what the web site was perhaps failing to address in terms of helping student learning. In this chapter we will presently discuss students' feedback and our results more specifically. We used an online questionnaire (http://richie.idc.ul.ie/tony/questionnaire_ma4704.html) to supplement the feedback we received from the TA evaluation with the small sample of students. We intended to garner some specific results with feedback from the class group in general about instructional and usability aspects of the site. We placed a link to the questionnaire on the course web site, and students were emailed and asked to fill in the questionnaire online. Students were asked if they had prior experience with statistics, and to what level they had previously studied the subject. We also asked students whether they accessed the site from home or from labs within the university, and if students were experiencing access problems. The questionnaire followed a number of themes of concerns, which were pertinent to our evaluation. First, we asked whether the ancillary supports were being used by students. Second, if they were being used, how frequently did students use them and, more importantly, how would students rate their helpfulness/usefulness. We also asked students questions relating to the frequency and nature of their collaboration with others, if any. Did they collaborate with peers around one computer while working through topics on the interactive web site? Did they use instant messaging or other forms of electronic communication, SMS (system management server) perhaps, to coordinate joint work for the course? We had a sizeable response rate: 101 of the 197 students responded to the online questionnaire.

We included a large text box at the end of the questionnaire to allow students to comment about the course in greater detail and more generally, and we finally asked them would they like to be taking more courses like MA4704 and why/why not. To supplement the TA evaluations, and to more specifically target feedback on usability aspects of the web site, we also asked students questions about functional aspects of the site like rollovers and note boxes, which are used for reminders and to display supplementary information about topics, and to explain difficult concepts or terms. We also asked students to rate the quality of the explanations on the site. We used Likert scales for this part of the online evaluation, diametrically rating the different aspects from poor to excellent. We can attribute the high response rate for the online questionnaire to a number of factors: 1) It was concise, 2) it was focused, and 3) students did not have to type too much and could expediently express reflections on aspects of the site, simply by clicking radio buttons on the online form. In assessing the instructional design of the course web site, we drew on aspects of Merrill's (2002) principles for instructional development. We endeavored to examine the following aspects: Is the courseware presented in the context of real-world problems? Are there techniques provided which encourage learners to integrate new knowledge or skill(s) in their everyday life? Following the TA evaluation sessions, we also held short semi-structured interviews with the three students to get their reflections more generally on the course and its instructional approach.

One of the main underlying motivators for designing the new course was the hope of the course leader that it might be possible to ground statistics for students. His concern is that statistics are too often reified or made too abstract for students, and that instruction in quantitative, analytic methods typically dissociates statistics from students' everyday lives, where it potentially could have a productive and profound impact. Moreover, he is concerned that this dissociation will continue into students' professional engineering careers and practice. Production management, manufacturing, and industrial quality control are domains in which statistical analysis and proper quality and safety control are crucially important. It might be possible online, using examples and animations of statistical problems set in real-world settings, to make the abstract and complex course topics more sentient, more concrete and understandable for students. Before we proceed to the results of our evaluation, we feel it is timely to show the reader this particular screenshot (see Figure 7.1), which illustrates the course's online contextualization of statistics.

Findings of Our Initial Multidimensional Evaluation

We found in our multifaceted evaluation that students can get through the topics online without really having to think critically about them. Asked about the web site, one of the interviewees said, "more searching questions

Figure 7.1

Online Animation of Statistical Aspects of Quality Control in
Injection Molding Process

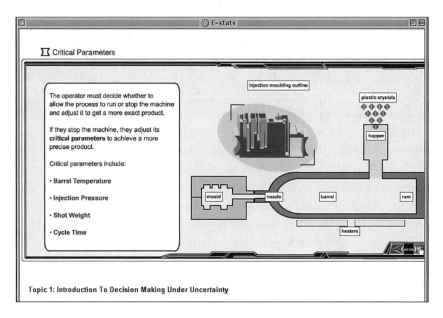

need to be asked." This is exemplified by the self-tests on the site, which loop continuously until the student gives the right answer. A number of the students we interviewed said that in the self-tests they often just kept trying different answers until they got the right one, without reflecting on why it was the right answer. The self-tests also create the fundamental usability problem that the user no longer has control—if a wrong answer is proffered the navigation buttons disappear. There is also the pedagogical issue that having to keep doing something until you give the right answer is overly pedantic. One of the interviewees commented, "It's like school, being forced to give the right answer." Of the online animations and the course generally, the students in the interviews and questionnaires reported that they found this a much more interesting and meaningful way to teach statistics. One student remarked, "This is a much better and more interesting way of teaching probe and stats than normal lectures which can be very tedious."

However, while students said the new course certainly gave them much more of a sense of how statistics can be applied in the real world, which should help them to integrate their new knowledge of statistics concepts and principles into their future internship or professional work, we found from the interviews, questionnaire, and TA evaluations that there is perhaps too little *synthetic* interactivity available for students on the web site. There is not enough, it seems, of a challenge and opportunity for students to actually or more authentically do (or *synthesize*, produce) statistical work. To illustrate the use of instructional technology to facilitate creative or synthetic interactivity, Merrill (2002) gives the example of courseware that involves the learner in using Microsoft Excel to prepare the previous month's sales figures for a fictitious friend's shop. The instructional technology facilitates the learner in working through a real-world problem. The courseware replicates Excel and the learner creates the workbook, enters the data, and creates the calculations and finally the financial report. In using the instructional technology, the learner is necessarily required to focus and reflect on spreadsheet and bookkeeping concepts. The courseware also supports instruction with nonexamples, which means the learner can make mistakes or take a problematic path through the instructional software but receives feedback on where he or she is going wrong. Another problem we found from our interviews concerned students' submission of answer sheets over the web. The response page only informed students that their data had been submitted, without telling them what they had submitted. Furthermore, when they received their results, they were just told their mark, and they were not told what they had gotten right or wrong, nor were they informed why they had gotten certain things right or wrong.

We would argue that the instructional design for the course web site, while generally very good in aesthetic terms and in terms of usability and clarity of explanations, could be changed to better support critical thinking about statistics. A possible problem with the current design is its potential to contribute to what Bell (2002) calls a "rhetoric of conclusions" (p. 499), and the seeming lack of challenge to students to actually do and reflect upon statistics. A possible idea might be that students do statistical work related to real-world settings online following Merrill's example, which becomes increasingly more complex as students progress through topics. It seems there needs to be more of a concern in the course design with eliciting critical reflection; less of a concern with getting students to give the right answers, and more with getting them to ask the right kinds of questions. In general, instructional artifacts should be designed to facilitate the development of learners' critical aspect and inquiry skills by supporting them in asking the right kinds of questions, and not with giving right answers per se (Hall & Wright, 2002; Koschmann, 2002). Importantly, we found that this change in the site design would need to be complemented with changes in the way feedback is provided on the web site. Students would need to receive feedback as they worked through topics, and not just feedback on what they are getting right or wrong, but *why* they are getting things right or wrong.

Redesigning the Site With Augmented Video Feedback

To help make the blended course support critical thinking more effectively, the first phase of redesign work following our portfolio evaluation was to enhance the self-test feature on the interactive web site. As previously noted, one of the problematic aspects of the original web site was its self-test assessment, which simply looped continuously until students proffered the right answer.

To enhance feedback and thus better support the training of middle managers, human resource trainers at the Boeing Leadership Center in St. Louis, Missouri, have designed an online instructional application that employs interactive narrative (Yamada, 2002).

The Boeing interactive narrative application employs digital video. Produced in conjunction with a small Hollywood movie company, the video snippets or vignettes on the online instructional site tell the story of a publishing house and a number of the people working there, and the various people issues that arise in their interactions with one another. The characterization of the employees in the publishing company is noteworthy: There is a colleague who is nearing retirement, and he does not want to upset things for fear he will jeopardize his pension; there is an ambitious and precocious new male employee, and a brilliant female colleague who has been recently promoted to the position of senior manager within the company. The different characters interact with each other in different ways, and such issues as gender discrimination and ageism arise among them. As part of their instruction in people management skills, trainee middle managers at Boeing watch this drama unfold online. The online drama is used as part of a blended learning course in concert with more traditional co-located and face-to-face instruction and discussion.

The trainee managers can also change the story so it unfolds in multiple different ways, and they can ultimately alter the ending of the story. By clicking on characters at certain points in the video, the managers can freeze the video frame and hear an interior monologue from the character they have clicked on. This digital soliloquy tells the trainee what the character is feeling and thinking at that particular time in the story. The application is compelling because it enables the trainee managers to see the results of different confrontational and problematic scenarios within a corporate setting. It also enables them to see the effect of different courses of action on different types of employees, which might be considered representative of the working population generally.

We explored using interactive digital video narrative to enhance the problematical self-tests on the web site (see Figure 7.2). We endeavored to develop an augmented, more enriched means by which to present students with feedback, which would help them to visualize and understand why they were right or wrong, and not just whether they were right or wrong. We also wanted to keep with the ethos of the course, which was to try to contextualize statistics in real-world settings.

We aimed to emulate, somewhat, the digital video application at Boeing. We explored using interactive narrative to enhance the problematical self-tests on the course web site. We consulted four students, two female and two male, and asked them, if they were to choose, what kind of interactive story would they like on the web site. These students responded that the characters should be people of their own age, people with whom they might be able to

Figure 7.2

Limited Self-Test Before Redesign

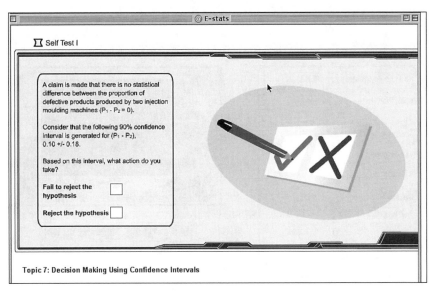

empathize. They also remarked that the characters should appear to be comparably wrong, so as the students got a question or questions wrong, the characters in the story would also get them wrong and require a commensurate level of additional help. Otherwise, the students felt the application could potentially make them feel even less confident about statistics.

While we principally aimed to enhance students' understanding of why they were right or wrong, and to avoid Bell's (2002) rhetoric of conclusions, where students have a repository of right and wrong answers but do not know why the answers are right and wrong, we also wanted to be able to provide some form of nonexample instruction, where students can see why a particular logic and particular answers/results are erroneous.

After consultation with the students, and also taking our design constraints into account, we finally decided on an interactive narrative, which would involve a central character called Johnny. Johnny is starting his internship with a manufacturing company, and he has been assigned to work in quality control. He struggled with statistics in college and now he has the unenviable task of working with them practically in a pressurized work environment. Furthermore, he has a less than understanding boss.

In the first phase of the web site redesign, we focused on enhancing the self-test for standard deviation (see Figure 7.3).

Figure 7.3

Johnny's Uncompromising Boss Assigns Him the Task of Assessing Standard Deviation on the Factory Floor

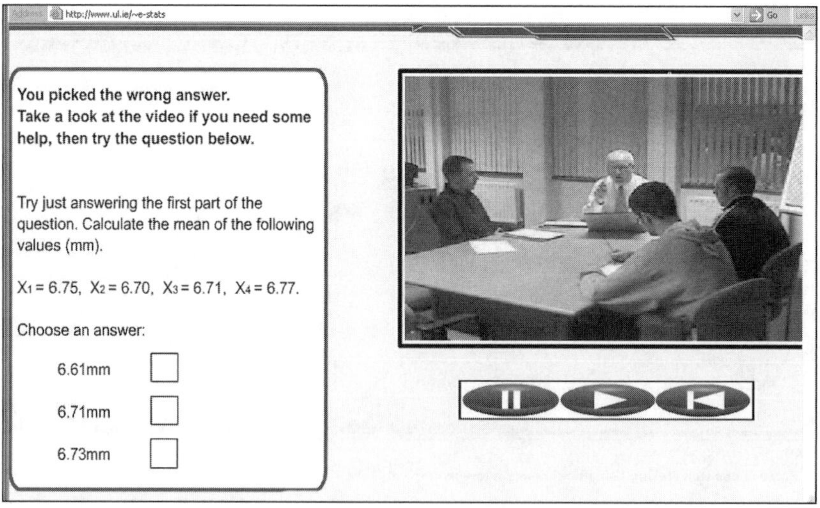

With the addition of the interactive video on the web site, if a student got a multiple-choice question wrong, a video would play depicting Johnny experiencing problems in using standard deviation to assess the quality of product samples at work. If the student continued to get questions wrong, Johnny's story would unfold, with the vignettes showing him asking colleagues at work for help. Depending on how poorly the student is doing in the self-tests (indicated by their providing consistently wrong answers), the vignettes become more rudimentary, as Johnny—in a kind of virtual empathy with the struggling student—asks simpler and more basic questions to try to figure out the application of standard deviation in appraising the quality of production processes in a factory. Students can pause or stop the video, and they can also exit the loop of explanatory vignettes once they are ready to answer the original self-test question, whereupon they can proceed in the course.

We designed the video script to follow a branching logic, which broke the topic down further, depending on the level of difficulty experienced by the student completing the self-test. We used Macromedia Director 8.5 to create the interactive online video application.

We integrated and tested this interactive narrative feature with the new class of students taking MA4704. On this occasion, we used the TA protocol and a web mail survey to garner feedback. We conducted the TA evaluation with four students, and we received a roughly similar response rate to the email questionnaire that we received with the online form in the original evaluation of the MA4704 course (spring semester 2003: 108 students from a class of 188 responded).

Generally, from this evaluation of the interactive digital video feature, we have found it provides a more informative, enjoyable, and motivational way for students to negotiate the online self-tests. Evidently, it provides students with greater encouragement and support to think critically about the given statistical problem. One student remarked, "I really liked the video. It was more fun than just reading text or animations. I didn't really find any difficulty with standard deviation, and was able to easily answer the online assessment, but I felt the video still helped me to understand it better."

REFLECTIONS AND CONCLUSIONS

In this chapter, we have endeavored to show how digital video can be used to enhance the feedback provided to students engaged in online assessment.

We have ascertained two key findings following from our iterative development and evaluation of the novel blended course.

Our first finding concerns the design of digital content for online assessment. We contend that semifactual digital dramas, like that of Johnny applying standard deviation in the factory, have a lot to commend them in enriching students' assessment online. These online narratives can help to maintain student motivation, especially where they are grappling with difficult concepts. In our initial evaluation, students found it particularly unhelpful and off-putting that the online feedback did not tell them why certain answers were right and why others were wrong. The dialogue between characters in the online video provided much richer feedback than the initial web-based multiple-choice assessment. Furthermore, the feedback was provided in a more compelling or interesting way. And by having an online character, Johnny, who was struggling his way through statistical problems, and with whom students could empathize, we seemed to significantly enhance students' engagement with the online assessment component of the novel course.

The portfolio of evaluative techniques that we used proved very helpful in enabling us to get a comprehensive picture of the effects of the novel course on a number of aspects of students' learning. Using a combination of heuristic or investigational techniques, we believe, proved more fruitful than had we employed only one method in evaluating the course. We believe that combined or hybrid evaluation techniques can prove very helpful in assisting those involved in designing e-learning applications to more effectively appraise complex blended learning scenarios.

We have focused, in the research presented in this chapter, on the use of interactive online video to enhance mathematical and statistical pedagogy. We would like to finally conclude with the contention that similar innovative approaches with digital video merit exploration in enhancing online instruction and assessment across subjects and disciplines.

Acknowledgments

We would like to thank Deirdre Hogan, Liam Brown, and all those at AMT Ireland, Plassey Technological Park, Limerick, Ireland, who were involved in developing the e-stats web site. We would also like to thank the many students who gave of their time and participated in our evaluation of the novel course.

8

Assessment Practices in an Online Lecture-Based Course and a Seminar-Based Course: Notable Differences

Ele McKenna-Byington

We give up control of answers on timed tests when we teach lecture courses online. If we administer timed midterm and final examinations, for example, we cannot seal students off from the world during examination periods as we can in face-to-face classrooms. We cannot ask students taking tests at home computers, or elsewhere, to place their book bags under the desk and talk to no one during a test, especially if a roommate is taking the same test. We cannot, in other words, stand guard over the answers to the questions we pose on exams. Some instructors handle this issue with tightened control over timing and accessibility to exams; they require students to take exams on campus.

For others, as it was for me, the perplexity of giving up control of access to answers in lecture course exams can lead to questions about the value of including timed tests (true/false, short answer, essay exams) in our curriculum in the first place. But if those tests evaluate students' ability to find rather than memorize answers, and if demonstrating an understanding of the questions is more important than trying to find correct answers, timed tests can work well, especially if what they evaluate is the end product of the teaching and learning.

However, my experience suggests that these tests work best when they are web-based and free from the restrictions of time and place imposed on testing in face-to-face classrooms. Also, my experience in teaching online lecture courses and writing seminars suggests that assessment practices that work in online seminars can transfer effectively to online lecture courses because both make use of interactive technologies, whereas assessments in face-to-face classrooms do not.

The purpose of this chapter is to share specific experiences of online assessment with those of you who, like me, are relatively new to web-based assessment. These experiences lead me to argue that web-based tests, partly because they come with time-and-place flexibility, can promote the goals of student-centered learning and provide unique opportunities for assessment of ongoing learning processes as students construct knowledge with other students and with their instructors. (For an introduction to recent—decades long—discussions in higher education about constructivist learning communities and other student-centered methodologies in both face-to-face courses and those mediated by interactive technologies see, among others, Brandon and Hollingshead, 1999; Bruffee, 1993; Comeaux & McKenna-Byington, 2003; Comeaux & Nixon, 2000; Romiszowski, 1997; Rovia, 2001; Shedletsky & Aitkin, 2001). But for that to happen there needs to be a revolution in our thinking about assessment.

In this chapter, I briefly discuss evolving online test formats, then note the many options that web-based testing can contribute to assessment practices. Next, I present the online lecture course I designed and taught in spring 2003 and, in the following section, the seminar that I designed and taught in fall 2003. The next two sections describe the specific tests and evaluations of group processes in these two courses, and the concluding section discusses the limitations of the context in which these courses are taught: entrenched university systems in the middle of fast-paced change and decreasing budgets.

EVOLVING TEST FORMATS

We don't need to give up all forms of online tests—from true/false to essay exams—because of a shift in control from instructor to students in test situations online, although we do need to be clear about the purpose of a particular test. If the purpose of a test is to provide feedback to students about how well they are constructing knowledge about a specific subject or acquiring basic methods of analysis during the learning process, that is, formative evaluations, then control and access to information during tests would not likely be important design factors. Formative assessments give students feedback about their progress during learning processes and are usually not graded or given nominal grade points for participation. Summative assessments, on the other hand, give students feedback about the end products of their learning processes. Often the only feedback is a grade on the product. End-product grades always complicate assessment, in class or online, partly because of the potential for cheating over grades. For this reason, devising a process of summative assessment can become a particular headache in lecture courses when we teach online and have to deal with a shift in assessment parameters, and have relatively large numbers of students enrolled in a particular course.

However, we gain control in other ways that make a difference in assessment practices. We gain control over timing of tests, which can revolutionize test formats. Room scheduling no longer controls the length and content of a test. We don't need to schedule online tests within a class period of fifty minutes or seventy-five minutes or even three hours. This flexibility means we can format test times according to the needs of the testing situation—times need not be limited by room scheduling during regular classes and during final examination periods. Test availability is easier to manage online. Students can take tests more than once and completely self-administer tests, if that serves the learning process.

The removal of both time and space parameters online blurs distinctions between tests and homework. All course work, including tests, is homework—or at least outside the physical space of traditional classrooms and outside the immediate control of the instructor.

The revolution doesn't end there. Online teaching affects assessment of note-taking skills. Students no longer have to take notes from our lectures online. Everything we present remains available to them for review from the first to the last day of the semester. This means that the ability to take good notes, that is, more or less accurately interpret what instructors say on the spot, does not have the same advantage online as it does in face-to-face classrooms. In other words, how well a student takes notes in class becomes irrelevant to the format of online assessments.

If there is an online record of everything an instructor presents during the semester, there is also a record of everything students write in response. All their online work is recorded. This written record makes formative assessments of collaborative work in lecture courses possible—in assessing, for example, participation in discussion groups, study groups, and writing workshops.

NOTES FROM THE TECHNOLOGY TRENCHES

In spring 2003, I needed to create formative and summative assessments for an online linguistics course I was teaching that semester in the English department. I had 70 students enrolled in two sections of that course and had a pressing need for help in managing assessment. The course delivery system for online courses at the University of North Carolina–Wilmington (UNCW), WebCT, provided that help.

Quiz Makers

A quiz-maker program, Respondus, works with WebCT to create and deliver online tests in various formats—true/false, short answer, paragraph, and essay exams. The program creates the format; the instructors create the content. We can revise the content anytime—two minutes before a test starts, after the test, or in another semester, if we want to do that.

Using WebCT and Respondus, I created a variety of web-based tests for assessing learning of central concepts and methods of analysis in my lecture course, administered at intervals throughout the semester. Some were machine scored true/false tests used as scanning-for-information exercises of particular readings, others were open-ended short answer, and still others were essay exams.

Only true/false tests can be machine scored. When machine scored, a WebCT option reports the scores automatically to the instructor and students. But when I must manually grade and respond to my students' answers on open-ended tests, WebCT still generates a report of those tests and makes them available to students online as soon as my responses are complete.

WebCT generates reports of all tests (with any feedback if that is included in the design of the test) and posts these reports as directed by instructors. If I want to delay a report of the scores for any type of test, machine or instructor graded, I have that option. I can hide a test until I am ready to make it available for a whole class or an individual student.

This web-based management of test scoring and reporting makes grading less labor intensive during the semester in classes with large enrollments.

Web-Based Delivery and Format Options

Web-based testing can provide options that only work online and simply are not feasible in face-to-face classrooms. The test availability option is one of these. If I elect this option, I can make a 75-minute test available online at times that are optimal for teaching and learning and that take into consideration, if possible, the hectic schedules of some of our students. A test can be programmed to remain available for any length of time, a few hours on the test date, or all day, or all week. The scoring and reporting of test scores, if this option is selected, occur after the availability period ends and all students have taken the test. Individuals have some control of when to take a test with this option.

Other options abound. For example, I can vary the format of tests, the point count, the length of the answers, the method of delivering the questions, how soon answers or responses are displayed after the test, how many times a student can take a test, and other choices too many to list here, all at the stroke of a keyboard.

Web-Based Communication Options

WebCT provides multiple channels for students to communicate with instructors about online tests—through chat rooms (in synchronistic time) and group or whole class discussion areas (in asynchronistic time), in addition to private messages using the class email system.

In the online lecture course, we used the chat rooms and the discussion areas—small group and whole class—to discuss particular assignments and tests. Question and answer sessions before a test work well in the class discussion area online. Students used the class email to communicate with me privately about tests and grades (and other personal matters that affected their test performance).

I posted tri-weekly messages on the home page announcements area, mostly to remind students to check the class calendar for upcoming tests and due dates for essay assignments.

I didn't schedule meetings with the students in my online courses on campus, but they could initiate a meeting at any time during the semester, especially if they wanted to talk to me about grades on tests or final essay grades, and, usually, one or two would. (A few students dropped in each semester during my posted office hours on campus just so we could meet face-to-face.)

One interesting note: Since students completed all tests and assignments online, I encouraged them to email or call me at home or at my office about technical or other pressing problems they had to deal with anytime during the semester. I directed them to call me immediately at home if those problems related to taking a test during the availability period for that test. With 70 students registered in this lecture course in spring 2003, I had only a handful of calls at home during the entire semester. This is, I'm sure, testimony to the efficiency of the online assessment system and to the increasingly skillful use of technology by our students.

A final word about the benefits of web-based testing in general. I found another assessment option particularly attractive—the My Grades option. Students can check my grade book, figuratively speaking, anytime during the semester. An up-to-the-minute report of grades for all tests taken (or missed, for that matter) and participation in groups is available throughout the semester to each student who wants to check his or her progress. They don't have to ask. They just click the My Grades link.

JOINING AN ACADEMIC COMMUNITY

In summer 2002, I designed an online lecture course for English majors, ENG 320: Introduction to Linguistics, and taught two sections of that course in spring 2003. Each section of this lecture course had an enrollment of 35 students. In summer 2003, I designed an online seminar course, ENG 306: Essay Writing, and taught two sections of that course in fall 2003. Each of those seminar sections had an enrollment of 20 students.

These were not my first experiences with online courses. I had adapted a composition course for first-year students, ENG 103: College Writing and Reading (Advanced), and taught that course online (again two sections) in fall 2000. In summer 2001 the online delivery system at UNCW changed completely, and I had to relearn the system to teach this course online in fall 2001 and 2002. Since I started my online experiences without even rudimentary knowledge of interactive technologies, most of the time I taught that course online I was learning to work with the technology and had little time to reflect or experiment or even adjust assessment practices. Fortunately, assessment practices don't change radically in writing seminars whether online or in face-to-face environments.

ENG 320: Introduction to Linguistics

This online linguistics course is one of four language courses in the English department curriculum at UNCW. All English majors with a concentration in teaching high school English or education majors in language arts are required to take this course. They are also required to take ENG 321: Structure of the English Language.

All other English majors can choose from one of the four language courses, all lecture courses, to fulfill this requirement. These courses include, in addition to ENG 320 and 321, ENG 322: Language and Meaning and ENG 323: History of the English Language.

Because both English and education majors need to take Introduction to Linguistics, the department offers three or more sections each year, all with an enrollment cap of 35. No section is ever underenrolled. Couple this demand with social and political pressure on the School of Education and the Department of English to produce more teachers to meet a shortage in North Carolina public schools, and, unsurprisingly, online sections of this course get the support of administrators as well as students—especially those commuter students who live an hour or more from campus.

Two objectives guide the course. One objective is to introduce students to linguistics concepts and methods of analyzing linguistic systems. Another is to apply this knowledge of linguistic concepts and methods to an analysis of their own language systems. We deconstruct different systems that make analysis of English possible—its syntactic, phonological, and rhetorical structures and methods for analyzing language in context. We also analyze children's language and their acquisition of oral and written systems. Many of the students in that course will be teaching children and young adults involved in the process of acquiring and refining skills in writing. We, therefore, make overt what are often covert assumptions, attitudes, and values about differences in the processes of acquiring oral and standard written English. The hope is that students will learn that what they value about their own language and the language of others, without reflection, might affect their teaching of language arts and high school English.

Assessment of students in this lecture course (and the other three language courses) has, traditionally and currently, been through in-class tests—a series of five topic tests spaced throughout the semester in the case of the sections I taught. In my online lecture course, collaborative assignments precede each topic test. Students work together in small groups to discuss their various interpretations of the class readings. In study groups, they complete problem-solving exercises and, in preparation for the topic test, collectively compare their understanding of a list of study questions before taking the topic tests. The work of understanding the questions is the most intense of the semester.

ENG 306: Essay Writing

This online writing seminar has enrollment capped at 20. It is one of two courses students can elect to fulfill a degree requirement for all majors in the English department. Like the linguistics course, it is offered frequently, is in high demand, and is never underenrolled. Professional writing majors enroll in this course along with literature majors, prospective teachers, and majors from other disciplines such as creative writing, film studies, and business.

The department administration wants sections of this popular seminar offered online for reasons other than high demand, although that is important. Online sections leave the computer lab free for sections of professional and technical writing courses—courses that are always in demand. These courses depend on using the lab to incorporate web-based instruction for professional writing purposes. Most of the professional and technical writing courses are web enhanced.

The teaching and learning in the seminar, online or face-to-face, is organized around the analysis and production of four loosely defined essay types: personal, narrative, critique, and personal for professional purposes (the type of personal essay that accompanies a graduate school application, for example). The course objective is to refine and improve the writing skills of each student.

An electronic course pack includes published essays from great writers that illustrate the art of writing well. I encourage students to respect formula writing for specific academic and professional purposes, but encourage them strongly to experiment with content and form and explore complex and sometimes surprising relationships between content and form in their own writing, as well as to consider the possibility of art in their writing.

In this online writing seminar, students think specifically about the fluidity of language forms as opposed to formulaic forms for professional and academic purposes. We analyze the power and intricacy of creating implied messages. We also analyze practical choices in essay writing such as lead sentences as transitions and topic sentences; topic information chains; cohesion devices in paragraphs and essays; the value of short, pithy lead sentences and of mixing long and short leads; the finer points of style in constructing sentences; and ways to recognize and remedy common types of sentence structure problems. And they see the results of improving such writing skill in the examples of the published essays we analyze together. No matter how conventional or unconventional the overall form, the skillful use of language never varies.

Collaboration is central to the activities in this online writing seminar. Assessments of student writing are formative in the early stages of the writing process through the final editing stage. Only the copyedited draft of each essay assignment (the end product) is graded. Students are trained in formative assessment of their own and others' writing. They know the difference between formative and summative assessment.

ASSESSMENT ONLINE: LINGUISTICS

The teaching and learning processes in this course are organized around a course pack of readings and the analysis of five general topics: 1) constitutive and regulative grammar, 2) dialect differences, 3) features of oral and written language, 4) conversational analysis, and 5) factors of context that influence meaning.

Summative Assessments

Essay exams. Five essay exams spaced throughout the semester assess the end products of the teaching and learning processes in five topic areas in linguistics, and the results of these topic tests constitute the summative grades for the semester. Here's how the web-based tests work. They consist of five open-ended questions. Because they have had the opportunity to study the questions and prepare the answers before the test, students are directed to respond in paragraph form in well-formed standard written English. (Lists of sentence fragments or lists of phrases are not acceptable responses because they can't adequately fulfill the requirements of the assessment task. Also, words, phrases, or sentences taken directly from the readings have to be enclosed in quotation marks, and any quoted language longer than a short phrase has to be immediately rephrased in the student's own words.)

Each end-of-topic test is timed for two hours and is available online for 24 hours. This means that students can log in anytime during that 24-hour period. Once logged in they have two hours to write their responses to each of the five questions. They can only attempt to take the test one time during the test availability period.

The approach to testing in this lecture course takes a writing-to-learn approach to teaching, learning, and assessment. Before each topic test, I give the class a list of study questions to prepare for the test in small groups. They work together, online, to interpret the questions and discuss their responses. But the written responses to the questions have to be submitted individually. The tests do not measure the ability to memorize concepts and methods of analysis, but they do test how well students can articulate these new concepts and methods in their own words, in writing. The end product, besides testing how well they are internalizing the concepts and methods, tests their ability to write coherently about concepts and analysis. Discussing the questions and then writing polished responses to the questions in preparation for the tests help the learning process.

Studying the questions for the essay exams. I also set up a question and answer session on the class discussion forum where students from any group can ask for clarification and discussion of any part of any question. Anyone in the class can respond in the discussion forum during the question and answer period. I check this forum several times a day while the study groups are ongoing.

I direct the students to write their individually composed responses to the study questions after the study groups have met and they have asked and answered whatever clarification questions they need to ask or answer. I see this step as a necessary part of the learning process. On test day they post their prepared answers online, adjusting those answers to suit the particular focus of the question on test day. These are not major shifts in focus. In fact, most of the questions will be almost identical to the study questions. They can, and some do, choose to write their answers directly online and not participate in the group activities. These students can locate the information in the readings during the test but only a few can produce lucid responses in the time allotted. And they forfeit 25 participation points when they are absent from the study groups.

Grading. I respond to and grade each essay exam online and post the grades. I also post the study group points online. The grades are automatically reported in the students' My Grades report.

Formative Assessments

True/false exercises. Students complete 10 to 12 web-based true/false exercises throughout the semester. These are scanning exercises of selected readings at the beginning of a major topic unit. The student and I get feedback on how that first reading is working. The true/false exercises are available for two days, and students have two hours to complete the task once they log in. They can complete the true/false questions with the readings open on their desks at home in the middle of the night. Each exercise with 10 questions is worth 10 points. Missing two or more of these online tests can raise a red flag about how well a student is keeping up with the course material online.

Grading. The true/false exercises are graded automatically and reported automatically to the My Grades report.

Open-ended exercises. Students in the linguistics lecture course also complete open-ended exercises that analyze selected readings from each topic. The format here is short answer (which allows for up to 25 lines, but the instructor can vary the amount of available response space). The language of these responses is informal, with less emphasis on academic writing conventions. These tests have five questions for a total of 25 points. The points are awarded for participation rather than for correct answers. They are available for two hours and can be accessed anytime during a 24-hour period.

The tests have a limited range of possible answers. I post my response to each of the questions (as one possibility in that range) when I grade the exercise. Students only see my response when they check their answers after the test availability period is over and all scores are reported. The process is a bit like taking a quiz in a newspaper for which the answers appear upside down at the bottom of the page or on a following page. Sometimes there is debate over the acceptability of one answer over another that needs to be resolved. The debate takes place usually through the class email system and forwarded to the whole class or on the whole class discussion forum.

But before the open-ended exercises first become available, and because they involve interpretation, I introduce for discussion Ortega y Gasset's concepts on interpretation of meaning. Briefly put, although multiple interpretations of a reading are possible, some interpretations omit central ideas or add to the text ideas that cannot be located in the text. Not all interpretations are relative, in other words. An interpretation can miss the point or misread a point. On the other hand, an interpretation can add points that cannot be supported by the text. I also introduce Louise Rosenblatt's (1983) views on problematic interpretations. In her book, *Literature as Exploration,* she states, ". . . but we can arrive at some consensus about interpretations that are to be rejected as ignoring large elements of the work, or as introducing irrelevant or exaggerated responses" (p. 281). I even point them much further back to I. A. Richard's 1951 analysis of misreading in *Practical Criticism.* This discussion is not an add-on to the content of the course but part of the discussion of linguistics and language use.

Grading the open-ended tests. I respond to and grade the open-ended exercises online and the grades are automatically posted in the My Grades report.

Reading workshop group. Another graded activity is not completed in quiz-maker format but in groups online. Students meet in groups to respond to a set of discussion questions for particular readings during the semester (after they have completed true/false and short answer exercises) for collaborative analysis of those readings. They first divide the questions among the group members, then post, before the due date for the reading workshop, all the responses in their small-group discussion areas. On the day of the workshop, they discuss the responses from the whole group. Then they delegate to one member of the group the task of summarizing their group's discussion and posting that summary in the whole-class discussion area. They take turns at posting the summary. I respond, as I would in face-to-face classrooms, to the whole class in completing the analysis.

Grading the workshops. Each member of the group receives 25 points for participating in the workshop after I record a grade for the individual, input on a rough scale of 1 to 10. Anything above a 7 will receive the full 25 points. Points are deducted as the score on the scale decreases. I post participation points online, and those points are recorded automatically in each student's My Grades record.

ASSESSMENT ONLINE: THE WRITING SEMINAR

In the online writing seminar the semester's work is organized in four cycles. The cycle doesn't vary whether the class is online or face-to-face. The cycles of work repeat themselves in significant ways. Every cycle involves scanning exercises of published essays to begin the assignment, then analysis and discussion of those essays in reading workshop groups before brainstorming essay topics in the whole-class discussion area. Submission of drafts follow a predictable pattern: first drafts to workshop group; submission of revised second draft to instructor for review and suggestions for final revisions; then submission of final drafts for summative evaluation and grade to complete the cycle of writing and rewriting.

The grading system doesn't vary whether the class is taught online or face-to-face. The grade on each of the copyedited final drafts of the four essay assignments in this course is based on performance, that is, summative. The grade reflects the extent to which the objective for the course has been reached on each of those essays. Only the final draft of each of the four assigned essays is graded in this way. All other evaluations are formative.

The formative assessments in this online writing seminar included true/false scanning exercises and open-ended tests as described above in the lecture course assignments. They also included reading and writing workshops.

The interactive technology provides a unique record of work in reading and writing workshops. This permanent online record of participation in the workshops made assessment easy. There is no place to hide online. If a student comes unprepared, the record shows that, and the record stays available all semester. This makes, for the first time for me, detailed formative assessments possible. Each student received points for attending the workshops, but also received more or less points for the quality of the reading analysis and the input during writing workshops.

What is interesting about writing seminars and why I include the discussion of the seminar in this chapter about assessment practices is that I adapted assessment processes I had used in the linguistics lecture course from the spring semester in the online writing seminar. And I will adapt assessment processes refined in the writing seminar the next time I teach a lecture course online. The web-based technology makes this cross-fertilization possible. I used web-based tests (true/false and open-ended paragraph form) in the writing seminar after realizing their potential for formative evaluation of student work from assessing that work in the lecture course. And although I used the discussion forum and chat rooms in the lecture course, it wasn't until I used them in the seminar course that I realized how much the technology helps me to make equitable assessments of student participation in these activities. There is a rare opportunity to observe the assignments in reading, writing, and discussion groups online. It is not possible in face-to-face classrooms to know exactly the extent to which students are participating in a slew of reading and writing activities during a busy semester. It is easy to do so online. Just as participation in these group assignments is available for scrutiny in writing seminars, it is also available in online lecture courses. This makes it relatively easy in a lecture course with 70 students to organize and manage group activities that work in either the discussion forum (asynchronistic time) or chat rooms (synchronistic time), since, in either case, written records are available.

Realization comes quickly to some students, who otherwise might be tempted to slack off, that participation counts online. All records are available by the stroke of a key. All I have to do is add up the points at the end of the semester.

UNIVERSITY SYSTEMS AND WEB-BASED TESTING

When we think of constructivist, student-centered teaching and learning, we generally do not think about lecture courses. Lecture courses are seen as a necessary evil to enthusiasts who advocate such teaching and learning. But a reliance on lecture courses as a mode of instruction has been around for a long time in university systems. And this necessary reliance is not going away anytime soon. Lecture courses at the UNCW make up a sizable number of course offerings for every department. Students, therefore, enroll in a lot of lecture courses. They need to take a variety of these courses during freshman and sophomore years, of course, to fulfill their basic studies requirements, although they can also enroll in a small number of seminar courses during the first two years. Upper-division students across campus also enroll in lecture and seminar courses, online or face-to-face, and a larger number of seminars are available to these students.

Typically at UNCW, the number of lecture courses and their enrollment patterns have not changed much over time. Enrollment is usually set at 35 students. In a few disciplines, some lecture courses have hundreds of students enrolled. Colleagues in the chemistry department, for example, regularly teach courses of more than 100 students. With increasing enrollments and decreasing funding, lecture courses are not likely to diminish in university schedules; instead, they are likely to increase.

Web-based testing, whether used in fully online lecture courses or web-enhanced courses, helps to manage assessment of students when the numbers are large but not in the triple digits. The first time I taught a lecture course online I was pleasantly surprised by the degree of flexibility I had in managing web-based tests—far more than managing tests in face-to-face classrooms bound by space and time. In teaching writing seminars online, I found that access to an accurate, written record of collaborative work during the semester made my formative evaluations more equitable for all students. Even in lecture courses, web-based assessment practices, because of the flexibility they provide, can promote the goals of constructivist learning communities whether a course is completely online or enhanced by the use of these technologies.

However, some underlying, sometimes deeply held, assumptions about assessment need to change to keep pace with an information age that dramatically alters who controls information and one that removes barriers of time and space in acquiring information. Some of my colleagues in the English department tend not to value standard tests even in lecture courses, especially if they are machine scored. In fact, they are deeply suspicious of anyone who administers true/false tests. But machine-scored tests as they are traditionally conceived are infinitely different from web-based testing. I used to believe that machine-scored test formats belonged only in the sciences, actually only in mathematics and chemistry, and not in upper-division courses in the humanities. That was before I discovered the versatility of web-based testing and its ability to support constructivist and other student-centered methodologies in lecture courses.

New questions about managing our assessment practices because of interactive technologies can lead to insights about how well we integrate assessment with changes in teaching and learning methodologies across campuses. If we merely try, in developing online courses, to fit traditional methods of assessment to this new medium (and bring students to campus so we can keep control of the questions to tests or limit the test time to thwart cheating) we could miss opportunities to revolutionize how we think about integrating teaching, learning, and assessment.

9

Online Teaching and Learning: Assessing Academic Library Skills

Marina Orsini-Jones

Child: "Teacher, what did I learn today?"
Surprised teacher: "Why do you ask that?"
Child: "Daddy always asks me and I never know what to say"
—Adapted from Papert, 1996, p. 14

Undergraduate students are not as young as the child in the quote above, but in my experience, often share this child's puzzlement toward learning. Independent learning is not a natural skill; it needs to be taught, as argued by Papert (1996). The use of technology, if carefully integrated within the curriculum, can help foster independent learning skills among students.

This chapter will illustrate how a subject-specific team—including staff from six different languages—collaborated with academic support services—staff from the Centre of Higher Education Development (CHED), the library, and computing services—in the implementation of online-supported curriculum change at Coventry University in England. The change was driven by students' feedback in an action learning and action research cycle as described by McKernan (1992).

- A problem was defined: Students complained that there were not enough books in the library for their studies.

- A needs-analysis was carried out: It was found that the books were there, but that the students could not find them because they did not know how to navigate the library catalog.

- An idea was hypothesized: The use of blended learning with WebCT would help students to learn how to navigate the library catalog and become more autonomous in their approach to academic searches and information retrieval.

- An action plan was developed: A team of languages lecturers, educational developers, and librarians worked at the development of a library skills unit to be included in a compulsory new skills module for linguists.

- The plan was implemented.

- The action was evaluated by all staff and students involved.

- Decisions for academic year 2003–2004 were informed by the reflection upon the actions taken in academic year 2002–2003.

The change process was based upon the successful integration of online assessment for information skills within the induction program for the students in the School of Mathematical and Information Sciences (MIS) carried out by the subject librarian for MIS with an educational developer from CHED (this development is described in Courtney and Patalong, 2002, and in Patalong, 2002).

The library skills information unit described here was created for module 143LAN Academic and Professional Skills for Language Learning, which ran for the first time in academic year 2002–2003. The module was designed to address the need to standardize the delivery of information and communication technology (ICT) skills across the languages group at Coventry University. It is meant to be a reflective module, where students think about the way they learn and transfer newly acquired skills to the other subjects that they are learning. It is compulsory for all level-1 undergraduates reading a language (or two) as a major degree subject at Coventry University and is meant to develop independent learning and personal development planning skills among undergraduates. This is a compulsory requirement for all courses in the United Kingdom Higher Education (UK HE) sector. In the language learning skills module students practice both language-specific skills (such as grammar learning processes, vocabulary acquisition, summary and essay writing, reading and listening, presentation skills) and more generic skills (such as library navigation, information retrieval, note-taking, ICT skills, and time management). Students are required to make regular contributions to the WebCT discussion forum and also write an electronic reflective personal portfolio of academic and professional skills progress.

WEBCT AT COVENTRY UNIVERSITY

Coventry University explored online learning environments between 1997–1998 with a dedicated Task Force for Teaching, Learning, and Assessment (Orsini-Jones & Davidson, 1999). WebCT was chosen from among the various products available at the time for its flexibility, its pedagogical soundness, and its value for money. It was also decided that WebCT would be the only online learning environment, that it would be used to enhance traditional teaching and learning methods, and that pedagogy, not technology, would be the driving force behind its implementation.

In order to make change easier for staff and students, a standard module template of WebCT facilities was created for all modules in the summer of 1999. WebCT induction is provided for all students, delivered by other expert students in collaboration with lecturers, liaising with the WebCT administrators, during induction week at the end of September. All new students receive a hard copy of the WebCT Online Learning Guide in their induction-week pack and can access further WebCT help online.

The online learning environment, which is Coventry University's in-house-designed portal, provides access to all the WebCT web sites within MyWebCT, where students will normally be able to access nine web sites: eight modules, plus a course web—in the UK HE context a module means a unit of a course, and at Coventry University students normally take eight modules per year.

While all modules are supported by a WebCT web site, there is no compulsion for lecturers to use WebCT. The academic year 2002–2003 statistics on use showed that the uptake of WebCT among lecturers in the six schools at Coventry University averaged 47%. WebCT must therefore be seen within a context of blended learning (Hofmann, 2001), as the majority of modules are still delivered face-to-face and WebCT provides an extra line of support for students (Davidson & Orsini-Jones, 2002; Orsini-Jones, 2003).

The Coventry University use of WebCT is seen as exemplary within the UK HE sector and was mentioned in an influential government report on higher education as an example of good practice in flexible learning (Department for Education and Skills, 2003).

> Coventry University runs an online learning environment, based on WebCT, which provides resources and learning management support for students in six different schools of study. Students can access a wide range of online study tools: lecture support resources, interactive quizzes, discussion areas for contact with fellow students and tutors, study calendars, assignment dates and study skill support. (Box J section, ¶ 1)

WHY AN ONLINE LEARNING ENVIRONMENT TO DEVELOP ACADEMIC AND PROFESSIONAL SKILLS?

There is evidence (Davidson & Orsini-Jones, 2002; Warschauer & Kern, 2000) that using an online learning environment can enhance students' learning experience. This is because networked-based learning allows students to (Davidson & Orsini-Jones, 2002):

- Find more opportunities to plan their discourse

- Reflect on their production

- Compare their production with that of their peers and their tutors

- Share electronic knowledge

- Feel that they share a more democratic setting with their tutors who become their peers in discussion forum

- Acquire useful transferable skills

The fluid role evolving environment (FREE) model (see Figure 9.1) represents the kind of role exchange that is brought about by the use of an online learning environment (OLE) such as WebCT. The students' contribution to the curriculum can become permanent and visible from one year to the next in a constructivist cycle. WebCT stimulates a continuous, healthy re-think of the lecturers' teaching, learning, and assessment policies in view of students' feedback. Attitude and motivation are important attributes in this integration model: Both tutor and learner are required to be reflective and responsive. It also requires a willingness on the part of the tutor to accommodate some degree of unpredictability, which is inherent in allowing the learning material to evolve (Orsini-Jones & Davidson, 1999). The visibility of their contribution can also encourage reflection among students, which makes the use of an OLE ideal for the teaching of a module like the skills one, which embraces a heuristic, process-based approach to learning.

Figure 9.1

The FREE Model

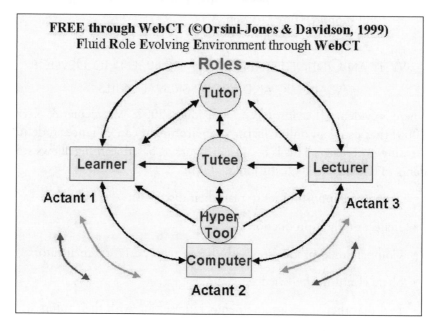

The introduction of an OLE within the curriculum must be thought through, as it is not inherently interactive, and lecturers and students need to collaborate in the construction of the virtual space to make it meaningful. The tool (see Figure 9.1) has now become a hyper-tool, but it still needs the mediation of careful learning management to successfully engage learners, particularly if learners are undergraduate students in their first year of studies, who can find independence and autonomous learning a challenge. Technology does not automatically lead to autonomy. As already mentioned in the introduction, learning, as Papert (1996) puts it, is an art that must be taught. Students should therefore be supported in:

- *Taking responsibility.* Thinking about what they are doing and why

- *Planning.* Setting targets and identifying the means to achieve them

- *Reflecting.* Thinking about what they have done, are doing, and are aiming to do

Blended learning can take many forms (Valiathan, 2002). In the case of module 143 LAN, it is meant to be a mix of methodologies and resource tools and assessed through a variety of methods.

This chapter focuses on assessing the ability to navigate the online library catalog and the library databases in support of language learning. This is assessed via the tailor-made information retrieval library test and counts for 30% of component 1 of the module mark (component 2 being the electronic language portfolio).

BUILDING AN ONLINE SUPPORTED LIBRARY INFORMATION RETRIEVAL UNIT TO DEVELOP ACADEMIC SKILLS

The aim of the information retrieval unit of the syllabus for the skills module is for students to be able to demonstrate the ability to navigate the online library catalog and the library databases in support of language learning. Following the analysis of students' feedback in the module evaluation questionnaires for language-specific modules in 2001–2002, it was decided, in discussions between language tutors and the subject librarian for languages, that the three following areas of information retrieval would be prioritized:

- Coventry University's library catalog

- Internet gateways such as the Coventry University's library web site

- Electronic databases

It became obvious from the beginning that the lecturers involved needed training and that the collaboration was vital, both because the library catalog was new and because the subject librarian had underestimated how difficult it was to navigate for academic members of staff (i.e., not from the library). The agreed action plan consisted of the following:

- Customization for languages of the information skills library navigation units designed by Patalong (2002) for MIS; timescale: April–July 2002. A whole suite of electronic tutorial materials was designed to be uploaded into the WebCT Contents area:

  - Creation of new database tutorials (the databases used for MIS were irrelevant to languages)

  - Creation of practical exercises, for face-to-face tutorials in the computer lab in the library, including a languages-specific treasure hunt in the library

  - Creation of a suite of multiple-choice test questions to be uploaded to the WebCT Assessment Area for both formative and summative assessment.

Structuring the Delivery of the Information Unit in Blended Learning Mode

It was agreed that the face-to-face library sessions would be team-taught: Both the subject librarian and myself would be present and we would also have the help of a technician if needed in some of the sessions. We also decided that there would be:

- Two two-hour sessions for two consecutive weeks in the library computer training suite

- Four more hours of practice in the face-to-face sessions outside the library

- Library-related content available on WebCT from the beginning of the term (September 2002)

- Three formative online practice tests available on the WebCT assessment area four weeks before the test

- Three summative online tests on a timed release for the date of the test

Planning, Designing, and Delivering the Online Tests on Information Retrieval

Assessment is the thorniest area in learning and teaching. When designing assessment tasks I am very aware of Boud's (1995b) claim that students can escape bad teaching but they can't escape bad assessment. Also, in my experience, undergraduate students have become more aware of assessment issues in the last few years—possibly because of the introduction of fees in the UK HE sector—and are quick to spot inconsistencies and unfairness (Race & Brown, 2001).

Because of the nature of the material being taught, we opted for multiple-choice tests and decided that the multiple-choice online assessment should be an open electronic book, in keeping with the heuristic, process-based nature of the module in question. To us, and to our colleagues in languages, the aim of this assessment task was not to penalize students if they could not find information about a book in the library, but to encourage them to see the library catalog as a useful and user-friendly tool for information retrieval. In doing so we also maximized the use of the resource area within WebCT, leaving it open to students to use during the test, so that they could become familiar with the direct internal links to the library catalog and web site from within their WebCT skills module's web site. We also agreed that students should be given open access to the contents area of the module containing the practice exercises and guided step-by-step tutorials on library navigation. We decided that six tests would be created, of which three would be formative practice tests (20 questions each) and three would be summative (10 questions each). The three summative tests would cover each of the areas of information retrieval that we had planned to teach: library catalog, Internet gateways, and electronic databases (see Figure 9.2).

This was a new development; therefore, it was not possible to predict exactly how students would interact with the online assessed test. It was also a first for me. Although I had designed formative online tests before, I had never had the courage to administer summative ones based on the hearsay knowledge that many things can go wrong. In this respect, it was very useful to time the formative online practice tests four weeks before the assessed one took place to enable students to provide feedback on the questions. They immediately spotted some ambiguities. Thanks to their feedback it was possible to rectify the latter before the summative test took place.

Figure 9.2

Open Web Online Test

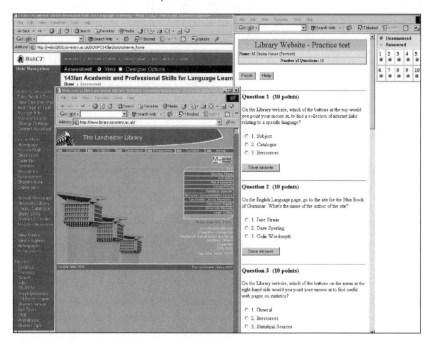

Despite all the joint planning something did go badly wrong 10 days before the date of the summative assessed test. While practicing the formative tests the students discovered that the Coventry University link to the database that the test had been designed for, Web of Science (now Web of Knowledge, http://wok.mimas.ac.uk), had stopped working. This required quick thinking on our part and a change in the format of the test. The solution to this problem was a compromise. I decided to redesign the test and administer one that was part online and part off line (see Appendix 9A). It would include an open-ended question on content-specific information about a contemporary aspect of the country represented by the language the students were studying. Students had to retrieve such information with a search on the full-text database Proquest Newspaper (http://www.il.proquest.com/proquest/), rather than an online test on databases, which could be answered in electronic format in Word or on paper and would provide me with a fallback position in case the server crashed on the day of the test. I also decided to allocate 50% of the mark to the two online sections, with 10 questions each (library catalog and library web site, 25% each) and 50% to the second, new part. The first major drawback of the change was that half of the test now had to be marked manually. The second was that I had not left enough time for students to practice the new task. In order to avoid further problems, the delivery of the test was very thoroughly organized.

- A WebCT expert was asked to be present on the date of the test so that any problems could be rectified immediately (and they were, as some did occur).

- The computing services unit was alerted that an online test was going to take place, to make sure that the server would not let us down (and it didn't).

- The faculty's technician was asked to service the computer laboratory that we were going to use in the library, to make sure that all stations were in working order (and they were).

- The subject librarian was asked to provide us with some temporary student IDs in case some students could not access WebCT (students can be blocked for library fines and cannot access the system if they are).

- All students were provided with hard copies of the online questions, just in case something went wrong.

I asked the students to post their feedback on the assessed online test in discussion forum just after its administration. The messages showed that on the whole students were happy with the tasks set, but that there had understandably been a bit of anxiety about the new section of the test. This was confirmed by the results, where most students scored very high marks for the online multiple-choice tests but comparatively lower marks for the open-ended database reflective task. The students who received the worst scores, in terms of results for the new section, were mainly the ones who did not attend regularly, as they missed the vital session in which I explained the new format of the test, and/or those who did not read the discussion messages on WebCT that explained the change. The students' feedback about the third section and the low marks obtained for it made me realize how ill-prepared they were for this open-ended section in comparison to the online test. On the other hand, it must also be pointed out that students obtained such excellent marks for the two multiple-choice online sections that this compensated for the lower marks for the new section. The most pleasing outcome was that all students appeared to have improved their information skills in comparison with their initial self-assessment in the skills audit that they had completed in October. I was particularly pleased with the marks of some more mature part-time students who had started the module with no ICT knowledge whatsoever.

STUDENT FEEDBACK ON WEBCT USE FOR MODULE ACADEMIC AND PROFESSIONAL SKILLS FOR LANGUAGE LEARNING

Student evaluations of the learning experience were sought in a variety of ways, using both qualitative and quantitative methods, namely (Orsini-Jones, 2003):

- Weekly reflections on WebCT (staff and students)

- Two focus-group interviews (Krueger, 1994), with two self-selected groups of students (12/41)—the transcripts were analyzed in collaboration with students employed as research assistants taking the module

- Discussion messages compiled and analyzed in collaboration with student research assistants

- Standard anonymous questionnaire in hardcopy (36/41 returns)

- Standard anonymous electronic questionnaire on WebCT

- Feedback at Course Consultative Committee, which students also posted to me on WebCT

- Discussion with colleagues involved in the teaching of Level-1 modules

- Interviews with staff on perceived improvement in level of skills among first-year students

- Qualitative and quantitative analysis of initial skills audit administered to students in October against performance on information retrieval test

- Pass rate on the online test

Although not all the questions in the interviews and questionnaires related directly to the online tests in particular and the use of WebCT in general, it was possible to extrapolate comments about both in order to evaluate the way in which students had experienced the online environment and tools. In the focus-group interviews students were asked open-ended questions mainly related to the effect that using the WebCT web site for the module had had on their confidence building in academic and professional skills and on their attitude to learning in general and to learning in their language-specific modules in particular. The transcripts were analyzed using the software package ATLAS.ti (Muhr, 1997), a workbench suitable for the processing of qualitative data. Two students were employed as research assistants and discussed with me the codes to use to classify the primary data. The codes directly related to WebCT that emerged from the analysis were benefits of WebCT communication, confidence building with WebCT, and limitations of WebCT.

Benefits of WebCT

Students found both discussion forum and module mail very useful to communicate among themselves and with me. Many students commented that using WebCT communication tools cemented their feeling of being part of both a learning community and a social community. Student representatives had, for example, used WebCT module mail to canvass opinions for both this module and others in preparation for the Course Consultative Committee, while other students had used module mail to organize social activities for all the members of the group.

Confidence Building With WebCT

The second set of positive comments related to the enhancement of students' confidence levels on the course thanks to WebCT's communication tools and contents area. This was mentioned with particular reference to the information retrieval unit illustrated in this chapter. Students were particularly appreciative of the amount of time that they were given to practice the formative online tests. Peer learning featured strongly as a positive aspect facilitated by online learning. The transcripts also confirmed what was found in previous studies (Davidson & Orsini-Jones, 2002): Shy students appreciate the fact that they can ask the tutor or their peers a question in module mail without the fear of public exposure if they have not understood something.

Limitations of WebCT

As for the limitations of WebCT, some students commented that:

- The amount of postings in discussion can be daunting and put off people from engaging with it.

- Text-messaging is faster for communication purposes.

- It is frustrating that some tutors use WebCT and others do not.

- WebCT is not as user-friendly as other ICT applications; it looks dull and can be slow and cumbersome.

Students did, however, suggest changing the order of the units on the syllabus and teaching information retrieval skills earlier in the term. They also felt that the assessment weighting was too heavy (30%) for a first test taken in the first term. These remarks were discussed and evaluated by staff and actions were taken in academic year 2003–2004, when the syllabus was completely revised.

ISSUES, CHALLENGES, AND LESSONS LEARNED

As with any development based upon technological innovation, we encountered a few problems. I often repeat that ICT developments are not for the faint-hearted.

First, there was the issue of the time scale, as the subject librarian nor myself had been allocated extra time for the development. So, particularly when things went wrong, time was very tight. Second, there was the issue of the ICT training required by both of us to implement the project. The subject librarian required training in the use of PaintShop Pro, Dreamweaver, and WebCT, while I had to become proficient in the use of question design in WebCT, Respondus for WebCT, the library catalog, and some of the databases used. This was rewarding in terms of staff development, but yet again, very time-consuming. Third, it was rather challenging, at the level of content, to include materials from six languages (English as a foreign language, French, German, Italian, Russian, and Spanish) and not always easy to liaise with 10 colleagues to receive input about particular language-specific issues and or searches (see the test in Appendix 9A with reference to this point). Furthermore, there were no obvious choices for languages databases. Databases are inherently difficult to teach, with many varying interfaces and search modes. Our fear of information overload on the part of the students proved to be founded (based on students' oral feedback after the first library session). Moreover, it became apparent that the over-familiarity of the subject librarian with the library resources meant an underestimation of the difficulties which students and academic staff might encounter when handling specialized information retrieval tools. Added to this, there was the online database test fiasco. A lot of work had gone into the design of the test and more had to go into redesigning an alternative one. The lessons learned from the experience are the following:

• It is easy to create information overload when teaching with online material. In the future we shall break down the delivery into smaller chunks and limit the number of searches.

• Databases such as Web of Science are too difficult to handle for most first-year undergraduate linguists. In the future we shall only introduce Proquest Newspapers in Level 1.

• It is necessary to encourage students to carry out directed subject-specific searches: liaising with other colleagues in languages is fundamental to support this, to create links and integration between the skills module and the content of the language specific ones, otherwise students will not see the skills module as relevant to their studies.

• The biggest weakness highlighted by the new section of the information retrieval test was the difficulty experienced by students in processing and analyzing the data found. More time needs to be spent on developing students' critical and analytical skills.

• The danger of unforeseen technical problems should never be underestimated. Alternatives to online delivery must always be at hand in case something were to go wrong.

Despite the problems encountered, we still feel that this was a positive development. On the whole, we felt that both the information retrieval tutorials and the online test had been a success. We were also pleased that so many stakeholders had contributed to this success, as it was a rather unique example of collaboration and exchange between academic staff (languages group), support staff (CHED, library, Coventry business school technicians, computing services), and students. I also felt that I had succeeded in my aim to develop the tests in a constructivist way using the

FREE model (as noted in Figure 9.1), as the final online assessed tests were developed incorporating the feedback students' provided after taking the formative tests.

Using an online learning environment provides a unique opportunity to "fix" the actions while they are being carried out and allows tutors to share practice with colleagues while interacting with students. The 10 colleagues engaged with the module carried out virtual peer observation as teaching assistants on the WebCT web site. As for myself, the students' postings enabled me to reflect upon my practice but also to diagnose students' weaknesses on an individual basis.

The use of WebCT discussion added to the new experience the value of the students' post-test reflections that staff found very useful. The students' written reflections, oral feedback, and performance on the test itself have informed changes to be actioned in 2003–2004, as the module is meant to evolve every year as a result of staff/student reflections in an action learning and action research cycle.

CONCLUSION

This development required a lot of commitment but was extremely rewarding. The feedback received from students and the work they produced for the module, both in the information retrieval test and in their electronic reflective language portfolios, seems to indicate that a tightly managed use of an online learning environment such as WebCT can promote reflection, encourage independence, and enhance the learning experience of undergraduate first-year students.

Appendix 9A
The APS Online Test Guidelines

Academic and Professional Skills Test, 1 12/12/02, FL109

Time: 2 hours
The use of the textbook (unmarked) is allowed.
This test counts for 30% of the module mark and reflects the MID learning outcomes 1, 4, and 5 (according to the task chosen in section 3). The full MID for the module is available at the MID home page. The learning outcomes are also reproduced in your module handbook. The test consists of three sections:

Section 1: The online test on the library website on WebCT, which will count for 25% of the mark for this test.

Section 2: The online test on the library catalogue on WebCT, which will also count for 25% of the mark of this test.

Section 3: This counts for 50% of the mark for this test. You must choose one of the following tasks:

A) **A search in the newspaper database Proquest** on one of the topics below. You must reflect on what you found, explain how you found it, how it was relevant (or not) to your chosen topic, and provide FULL BIBLIOGRAPHICAL REFERENCES for at least two of the relevant sources found. **A short summary in your own words of your favorite source MUST also be provided.**

OR:

B) **A search with the browser Google** (http://www.google.com) on one of the topics below. You must reflect on what you found, explain how you found it, how it was relevant (or not) to your chosen topic, and provide FULL BIBLIOGRAPHICAL REFERENCES for at least two of the relevant sources found. **A short summary in your own words of your favorite source MUST also be provided.**

In Section 3, remember to report all bibliographical details about your sources using the Harvard referencing system. Remember what was said in class about providing references for WWW sources. Treat Proquest as a WWW source, but describe the steps taken to make use of it. **You must**

write at least 250 words for the chosen task in Section 3; short answers
will be penalized. Type the answer for Section 3 in Word and submit it as a
Module Mail WebCT attachment to Marina Orsini-Jones. Suggested topics which can be searched for Section 3A and 3B (you may suggest a different one, subject to MOJ's approval, raise your hand and ask):

English
Life in Coventry
British society today
Life at university
English language (grammar, slang, vocabulary, variety, change)

French
Family life in France
Religion—religious beliefs in France
Social classes
Paris/the provinces
The French language (history, evolution, regional accents)

German
German geography
Germany today
Germans today
The German language
The world of women in Germany

Italian
The Italian family
Italian fashion
Italian geography
Italian food
Tourism in Italy
The Italian language

Russian
The Russian alphabet
Russian society today
Russian food
Tourism
Sports and leisure in Russia

Spain   .
Present-day Spain
The Hispanic world
Spanish today
The family in Spain
Young people in Spain
Tourism in Spain

10

Computer-Mediated Communication as an Instructional Learning Tool: A Course Evaluation

Bolanle A. Olaniran

Computer-mediated communication (CMC) consists of electronically mediated communication systems (e.g., email, computer conferencing, video conferencing) that facilitate interaction among people. The goal of this chapter is to present findings from a case study (i.e., a course) using a combination of CMC and face-to-face (FtF). From the design, the students were able to compare both media as to how well the media were able to achieve the course objectives and meet students' preferences. The comparison is essential for addressing how CMC complements the traditional method of instruction and facilitates student learning. The next section presents a description of the instructional design.

DESCRIPTION AND ANALYSIS OF INSTRUCTIONAL DESIGN

Results from a graduate course in the Department of Communication Studies, COMS 6303 or Seminar in Interpersonal Communication, provided critical assessments of interpersonal communication in CMC and FtF media in terms of learning and other instructional issues. As the instructor, I served as the moderator for the course. The course utilized a combination of CMC and FtF discussion (i.e., CMC/FtF condition). Twenty-three students were enrolled; however, 19 completed the course. The course took place during the summer term, a four-week period at

Texas Tech University. Prior to the evaluation study, a preliminary course using the combined CMC/FtF media was conducted to anticipate and eliminate problems associated with this instructional method.

The CMC Systems

The instructional design consists of a CMC system that features the VAX mainframe terminals to which modems and Ethernet cables link other microcomputers. The communication protocol chosen for the computer mediation consists of Vaxnotes and the electronic mail provided by the system. Vaxnotes is an electronic conferencing system that enables participants to log on to a conference and add their contributions. Vaxnotes is similar to the listserv system in that it allows individuals to participate in an electronic meeting using any of the following functions: reading others' comments, typing or attaching personal comments, editing, and printing hardcopy for later review. The Vaxnotes conferencing feature is more structured and easier to follow than the listserv because it allows the instructor to create the conference forum (i.e., file) in a central location and to control access to the conference. This mechanism is possible because of the editing privileges that give the instructor control. It also enables the instructor to capture all input by students. When a student enters a conference, he or she is notified and prompted by the numbers of unread new messages. Therefore, the users are not likely to waste time on messages they have read in prior sessions. In addition to Vaxnotes, students were issued regular email accounts at the beginning of the course to give them the flexibility of a one-on-one interaction with other students and the instructor.

Course Content and Designs

The graduate course consisted primarily of communication majors who are pursuing their master's degrees. Some of the students were teaching assistants in the department while others worked off campus in various organizations ranging from teaching to supervisory positions in the community. The course was aimed at introducing students to interpersonal communication media theories. Specifically, the course attempted to explore how theories influence communication practices and applications. Application is as essential as the awareness of theoretical principles of learning. It is evident that personal and organizational success to some extent depends on the ability to use technology and to work in electronic environments. Experiences with CMC may also help prepare students for future adoption of such technology and the contemporary global economy at large. The FtF portion of the course followed the traditional structure as the class met at regularly scheduled times for discussion of assigned readings and students' experiences with CMC. The following criteria represent the conditions in the seminar format: All course assignments and notifications were made and required to be turned in through CMC (either email or Vaxnotes) and specifically, assignments that were designed to generate interactivity were conducted through the Vaxnotes conferencing. Other individual-based assignments were conducted through email while announcements were posted in the general section of Vaxnotes. The CMC/FtF course design deviated from the one-dimensional design that focuses on either asynchronous or synchronous application of the CMC medium used in a previous study (e.g., Olaniran, 1995). The design of this course helped to simulate realistic settings where people using CMC also have access to other communication media for interaction with their co-participants. The CMC/FtF course design was intended to gradually ease users into the CMC process by reducing anxieties. The course design also recognized the need to reduce students' anxieties, which is necessary in dealing with the perception of loneliness that has been attributed to CMC in the early stages (see Moore, 2002; Ng, 2001). The design also allows students to compare and objectively evaluate both FtF and CMC media and their suitability for communication activities.

Training

As the instructor, I conducted CMC system training for students in three two-hour mass training sessions. Though the training was done in a short time period, the use of handouts and a hands-on format allowed students to learn about the technology (i.e., Vaxnotes), the course, and the procedures. For example, the training required students to enter into sample conferences by reading and attaching comments for other participants in an attempt to become familiar with the Vaxnotes protocol. I clarified the purpose of Vaxnotes and email along with their appropriate use. From this clarification, students learned the options of sending messages to an entire class, to a few people, and to selected individuals. Participants had ample opportunity to practice with the system by sending messages utilizing the appropriate option.

Task and Course Assignments

Emphasis was put on tasks that allowed for discussion and greater inter-activity in the course. To gauge the students' proficiency, students were given assignments that required them to email the instructor (e.g., definition of interpersonal communication at the beginning). Even then, students were asked to post their definitions on the Vaxnotes and continue to provide justification while discussing (either agreeing or disagreeing with other class members' postings). A major assignment asked students to discuss their perception of the CMC medium along the line of media richness claims and to address its implications for interpersonal interactions. Other assignments focused on the applied use of technology. The goal was to get the student to realize some of the potential uses for CMC outside the classroom. One of the assignments asked the students to discuss whether messages and interactions in CMC are socially cold or warm, especially given the fact that CMC does not support verbal cues. This was an ongoing assignment, where students were required to evaluate the technology in an attempt to determine whether time has any effect on students' arguments and perception of the technology medium. The information presented in this chapter will focus primarily on observation and analysis based on the first assignment and CMC use within the course. I hope that results from the interactive discussions in the Vaxnotes will assist other instructors on how to use CMC effectively in their respective courses.

To reinforce active participation, I restricted discussions concerning CMC assignments during class periods to only the assignment due on that day, and 25% of the course grade depended on the quality of participation. Activity was evaluated both objectively and subjectively. Objective criteria consist of factors such as the number of log-ins and the number of messages or responses posted in the conferencing forum of the Vaxnotes. Subjective criteria include the quality of interaction and the argument posted. This is measured by the relevance of the argument presented in the students' messages, how well the students provided a cogent argument using readings and relevant literature, and if the quality of the argument was indirectly based on how well individuals brought in their personal experiences with the technology. (See Olaniran, 1994, for similar quality evaluation criteria.) Participants were also instructed that failure to turn in assignments for reasons other than hardware problems would result in loss of credit. Data were gathered from transcripts from the CMC system that allows interactions to be captured for data analysis while FtF interactions were captured with a voice-activated tape recorder and transcribed.

CMC as an Instructional Tool
In examining CMC as an instructional tool, I focused on five issues facing educators regarding CMC and technology use in classrooms.

- CMC interaction pattern and perception of accountability

- Course management

- Reflective learning

- CMC structure/design

- Time effect and relationship development

A more comprehensive discussion of these issues is presented below and guides the way the study was analyzed and reported.

ANALYSIS AND DISCUSSION
I describe students' experiences in class settings in a way that captures the essence of their interactions and their perceptions of the course and the communication media. The transcripts from both the CMC and FtF portion of the data were coded and categorized by two research assistants. The transcription of FtF tapes was necessary as a measure to ensure uniform coding for both CMC and FtF (Olaniran, 1994). The findings are presented below.

CMC Interaction Pattern and Perception of Accountability
There is evidence of disparity in interaction patterns between the more competent CMC users and the new users. For instance, one aspect of such differences is in the area of icons and social cues. The literature suggests that icons (i.e., smiley faces) are used in CMC interactions to compensate for the lack of nonverbal cues (Lea & Spears, 1992). The CMC transcript suggested that more sophisticated users used the icons (e.g., ☺ ☹), whereas the less sophisticated users wrote out the expression that the icon conveyed (e.g., "I'm joking," "Just kidding," etc.) or avoided their use altogether.

The transcripts provided insights into perception and implication for accountability of messages. Accountability means those instances in which messages are directed at a specific person about his or her behavior or prior messages. CMC data indicated that messages were phrased in a way that holds other individuals somewhat more accountable than similar messages in FtF. For instance, the analysis showed disparity in occurrence of accountability: 107 episodes in CMC interaction compared to 15 episodes in FtF. In other words, 43% of CMC messages used accountability while about 1% of FtF messages did. Interestingly, accountability messages appeared to foster a greater sense of commitment from students. In the CMC environment, messages tended to be direct comments and responses to specific individuals, substantiated at length; individuals seemed to defend their positions more rigorously than they did in the FtF environment. This effect can be attributed to two factors. First, the text-based message and record-tracking feature of the CMC medium offers and preserves a permanent record storage. Second, peer awareness of students' messages could create expectation for greater accountability and consequently affect the level of commitment and participation. These factors are also present in FtF interactions, but are considerably mediated by "face-saving" strategies in which one attempts to avoid embarrassment. These strategies may explain the greater accountability found in the CMC medium. The difference can also be explained by the fact that CMC participants are less subject to evaluation apprehension (Olaniran, 1994, 1995) because criticisms do not have the same effect in CMC as in FtF due to the mediating role of technology. Comments that indicated accountability also tended to be correctional, and at times, seemed confrontational when illogical arguments were perceived. This pattern was seldom the norm in FtF discussions as comments were more general and with no direct reference to a specific person (e.g., hesitant). The following sample statements are typical of the accountability in CMC.

CMC:
Dan, I disagree with you on that. I don't think simply because you're a computer "guru" [that it] justifies your claim that CMC is a richer medium than FtF. After all, nonverbal message[s], which are essential to fill in the missing cues during interaction, are absent in CMC medium.

CMC:
Some of the people (i.e., Paul, Joe, Rachel) responding to this message have lost sight of what the topic was. It said in situations requiring more coordination, not just any given situation. For this reason I think FtF is the most effective way of communicating in tasks which need large amounts of coordination.

FtF:
I think FtF has more to offer for accuracy, because I can easily watch people's nonverbal [cues] and determine what is going on. Therefore, I prefer FtF medium . . . it is richer than CMC.

The preceding CMC remarks present situations in which students directed their responses specifically to a particular person or a group of people regarding their previous messages. In these episodes, while the messages seem to be holding Dan and others responsible for their previous comments, there is less likelihood for emotional conflict, the kind likely to occur in a FtF setting. A case in point is the following exchange in CMC.

First of all when typing on e-mail, DON'T USE CAPS. It means you are shouting and it is VERY ANNOYING to read.

Responses:
I am sorry for using all caps to write; I am new at this and I didn't realize it would cause any problems. Thanks for the insight!

Or:

Thank you for politely informing me of the inappropriateness of caps in this format.

Given the lower impact of evaluation apprehension in CMC, one could argue that there is an opportunity for greater willingness to participate in CMC discussion by participants. For instance, CMC transcripts indicate that students who generally refrained from contribution in FtF discussion participated more actively in CMC. As the examples above indicate, negative criticisms exist in CMC. However, when criticism occurs, it seems that it has less negative emotional effect than in FtF interactions (see Olaniran, 1994).

Also, the presentation style in CMC episodes suggests that poor argumentation or gross oversimplifications are not going to be tolerated. This idea may also give students the impression that they have to do more than just participate for the fun of it. The fact that one's name is attached to one's message may foster accountability in CMC, as other students are likely to put names and faces together at a later time.

Course Management

In CMC, students realized that they did not have to depend only on the instructor or their own ability to obtain answers to questions. That is, if a student needed certain information that was not readily available, the student could post a message asking for assistance. In all likelihood, there was bound to be someone who could provide an answer. Furthermore, a post-class evaluation question asked students to describe the usefulness of each communication medium focusing on three factors: 1) information resource, 2) information speed, and 3) information accuracy. The data was then coded accordingly. If the response indicated feelings of usefulness without any reservation, it was classified as "useful." When the response indicated feelings of resentment toward a medium without any reservation, it was classified as "not useful." When the information revealed either mixed remarks or no comments were offered, it was classified as "neutral." From the useful category, compared to 37% who preferred FtF, a greater number of the students (63%) reported that they found CMC to be a fast source of information. A major concern with the FtF condition was waiting until an instructor is available for consultation or until class to obtain an answer to a question. For information accuracy, a result similar to that of information speed was obtained: 74% considered information from CMC to be accurate when compared to 26% for FtF. The difference could be attributed to the fact that students indicated it was easier for participants in FtF to switch their stories or information at a later time, whereas the record storage capacity of CMC eliminated this option. In addition, information accuracy was perceived to be greater when more people provided similar answers than when an individual did. There was no major or statistically significant difference found between FtF and CMC media when perceived as information resources. As a matter of fact, a somewhat greater percentage of participants considered the

FtF medium to be a better information resource (i.e., 52.6% viewed FtF as a useful information resource compared to 47.4% in CMC). The degree to which the difference is attributable to the value placed on nonverbal cues is unknown. Therefore, it may be necessary for CMC users to establish relationships with one another and gain confidence in the system before proceeding in its use (Walther, 2002).

From my perspective, CMC shifted the burden of learning from the instructor to others (e.g., students and nonstudent experts) and allowed me to focus on other aspects of the course depending on the nature of the assignments. For instance, a considerable drop in the proportion of direct teacher-student FtF interaction was noticed relative to the traditional FtF course. Consequently, in CMC environments the instructor's role tends to shift from that of information provider to that of facilitator. The reduction in time, however, only affects interactions that call for an instructor's physical presence; general student-teacher interaction time increased as instructors have to spend more time reading student contributions and responding to each student's inquiries and postings. The data from the two media revealed that the proportion of students contributing to in-class discussion on a consistent basis was 56% for FtF and 79% for CMC, respectively. Often the instructor engaged in CMC conferences only to clarify disputes and to moderate the discussion process when students were getting off track.

Reflective Learning

The shift in the proportion of interaction between student and instructor in the classroom is believed to facilitate the learning process, specifically transformational learning. Thus, the use of CMC in teaching a course fosters the goal of transformational learning. Transformational learning (Clark, 1993) specifies three factors that must occur: 1) validation of prior knowledge (authenticity), 2) modification of prior knowledge (alteration), and 3) replacement of prior knowledge (complete shift). Therefore, the transformational learning process requires that one be allowed the opportunity to compare and contrast (i.e., experiential) previously acquired information with new or novel information before making an informed judgment as to what to believe. This process is facilitated through the direct communication process enhanced in CMC. Sample excerpts from the transcripts suggest occurrence of transformational learning in the course.

Halfway through the CMC/FtF course:
I honestly believe that FtF is the richest medium due to [the] presence of nonverbal cues and the immediate feedback; however, an interesting point was raised in class yesterday concerning the success people have enjoyed for many years writing letters. I don't think that letters are particularly lean; sometimes I get more of an idea of how my friends feel reading their letters as opposed to talking on the phone or in person. I think that CMC is very similar to writing letters, but better in that feedback is much faster. I am definitely seeing CMC in a brighter light since last week.

Some examples of replacement of knowledge:
I agree with Renee. My knowledge about CMC was zero, but the more I use it the more I am beginning to like it. I so feel as though your answers or statements are more thought out than what you would say in FtF, and you are more likely to say what you really feel.

Or:

As the class progresses I see myself changing my views about CMC. From the readings and discussions I have begun to value the possibilities that CMC has to offer. Not only that, I have begun to look at our messages in a new light. As I read them I can see bits and pieces of people's personalities show through. For example when some people forget to sign their names it's often easy to guess who it was (who you think it was). I have to admit I've been swayed . . . I am now readily willing to admit that CMC is thoroughly a medium of richness.

Or:

I have progressed through the normal stages of being totally afraid of using the computer to feeling relatively comfortable in using it.

At the end of the course, transcripts were analyzed for those statements that expressed willingness to change opinion and preference for either of the two media. It was found that 74% of the CMC/FtF class fell into the categories of either modifying their opinion or completely changing their opinion about CMC as a suitable communication medium. Twenty percent indicated clear preference for the FtF medium, while the remaining 6% were unclear or neutral about their medium preference. It is possible that the change in opinion of both communication media could be attributed to the course design. Nonetheless, the CMC and FtF format helped fortify the transformational learning experience by providing students with practical use of communication technology, providing students with the opportunity to verify and validate theories that applied to them. Such a learning process enhances greater knowledge retention than either theoretical or applied learning taken separately. In addition, the CMC storage feature creates a permanent record of class interaction to which students can return and self-reflect, a goal that I believe is difficult to accomplish in FtF interactions.

CMC Structure/Design

The use of both email and Vaxnotes helped to create a unique classroom setting. The forum in Vaxnotes alters the traditional student-teacher interaction because it is public and less personalized. At the same time, email enables students to engage in personalized exchanges and learning experiences with teachers and peers (Yu, 2002). Either participation style can be evoked anytime during the discussion process. That is, a student can simultaneously participate in a conference and decide to send an individual and personalized message to another student or the instructor without being disruptive. However, this is seldom the case with the FtF because an aside conversation other than one approved by the instructor takes away other students' ability to concentrate. Participants can log in and out of the two modes without missing any of the interaction process. Other benefits of CMC include the ability to overcome problems resulting from incomplete note-taking and absences from class due to the information storage and retrieval capability of the medium. The following are sample comments reinforcing this argument.

> I feel I'm not missing anything when I could join the discussion and read others' comments, knowing that I still have the same information the other people have.

> It's really cool to be able to print out the class discussion and insert in the class folder. It's hard to miss anything like you would if you're paying attention to [the] instructor's lecture and trying to take notes at the same time. This CMC stuff is just what the doctor ordered.

The potential benefits of CMC's storage and retrieval features for learning cannot be ignored. Similarly, the impact could also be detrimental. It may offer students the incentive to skip class discussion or procrastinate by postponing tasks until it is too late, resulting in poor performance.

Time Effect and Relationship Development

Initial anxieties were expressed about CMC in the beginning of the course, but they seemed to dissipate toward the end of the course. The reduction in anxieties can be explained by drawing from the innovation literature. Resistance to innovation is high during the early stages of diffusion of innovation because of fear and lack of knowledge about the innovation (e.g., Olaniran, 1994; Yu, 2002). Therefore, it is essential to develop some sense of interpersonal bonding among students in order for meaningful interaction to occur. The FtF discussion speeds the development of interpersonal bonding, which is believed to be helpful in mediating the degree of resistance that is associated with innovation processes. Time is also essential to help inexperienced students with CMC usage. Below is a sample remark that reinforces inexperience in CMC at the beginning of the course.

> I have not had much experience or exposure to CMC prior to taking this class. For this reason, I do not think I can give an objective opinion about which medium [FtF/CMC] is richer. I have always felt that FtF communication is richer than CMC.... Any other type of medium can not be substituted for FtF communication in its use and preference.

The combined media design was essential in simulating interactions similar to those found in most organizational settings, where members are often allowed to use multiple media for interaction. That is, participants should be given ample time in order to gradually help inexperienced users adapt to CMC. Thus, while people may be using the CMC medium, they are still able to interact via FtF. This design is essential for the success of a beginning course in CMC, especially in courses in which time is of the essence and the majority of students are inexperienced CMC users. The following comments reflect some of the changes in initial attitudes among students who were inexperienced in CMC.

> At the beginning of the course and for the longest time I thought that FtF communication was richer than CMC, but after using the system more and playing with the MUD I am more comfortable and I have changed my mind.

> Even without the ability of touching, CMC can provide everything that FtF does. Basically what I am saying is that I don't think that CMC is as difficult as I first thought or that FtF is that much richer than CMC.

> I viewed FtF as [a] richer and easier medium to use before I used a CMC system. However, after I used CMC I feel that in certain ways it was richer than FtF.

The comments above should not be taken to mean that students will become immediate converts to CMC, only that the potential increases with the approaches and strategies used, as few students at the end of the course still indicated a preference for FtF.

The use of the combined media approach in this study is believed to facilitate a steady change that allows students to be introduced gradually to CMC. Students do not have to feel like they are being forced to give up FtF for CMC since they are still able to rely on FtF when needed. Therefore, the combined media give students greater flexibility in course participation than either medium separately.

REFLECTIONS AND RECOMMENDATIONS

Course Design

The choice of using FtF, CMC, or a combination should depend on the course and the course goal. More specifically, attention must be given to environmental factors that constrain the decision. One of those factors is the length of the course. For instance, it appears that courses using CMC are difficult to conduct successfully in a short period because of the amount of time required for system learning in order to develop comfort with the system. Instructors are advised to allow themselves and students ample opportunity to bring about the learning process in a steady manner by providing adequate time for students to adapt to the instructional uses of CMC. Special attention must be devoted to this factor, especially when course goals include facilitating acceptance, skill acquisition, and adoption of CMC. A recommendation is that, when one is pressed for time, FtF-only might be the most viable option, especially with novice users. However, if time is a critical factor and using CMC is essential, a combined set-up (i.e., CMC/FtF) might be appropriate (see Olaniran, 1994). The argument often used against combining FtF and CMC is that the combination penalizes the geographically distant students. While this is true, recommendations here are for same-campus interaction and not distance education. Notwithstanding, a system that interfaces video and audio cues may help overcome this challenge.

The Changing Role of Instructors

Instructors' roles appear to change from lecturing to facilitating instructional goals with CMC in two critical areas: Feedback and personalized learning focus. Instructors, in their new role as facilitators, need to become more active in providing appropriate and timely feedback to students. Instructors would have more information to process in CMC than in FtF classes. This effect may be compounded by CMC's ability to support large numbers of active participants. Instructors would have more information to attend to as the volume of information in a CMC class outnumbers FtF (assuming similar size classes). Therefore, a strong commitment is required on the instructor's part to provide feedback to students' inquiries in order to maintain the flow of interaction. The need to facilitate active and meaningful participation among students may also require instructors to moderate interactions. That is, the instructor must engage in reflecting, paraphrasing, summarizing, and other activities to bring the class discussion into focus and to clarify guidelines for interaction.

Lessons Learned

In utilizing the combined media approach in classrooms, I learned several things. With students, as with many faculty, change in any form is a difficult process. This case study is no different. The lack of familiarity with a communication technology such as CMC creates anxiety for users to the extent that they needed time to adapt to the technology and develop a sense of comfort with it.

I discovered that commitment and dedication to the goal and content of the course is just as important as the novel idea of implementing new technology in the classroom. CMC requires planning; however, one cannot plan everything, especially with technology. Thus, an instructor must be flexible enough to address unforeseen contingencies that are likely to arise in the course of using the technology.

I also learned that no matter how good a technology medium is, it requires time to bring about the desired effect. Therefore, incorporating technology in the classroom for the sake of using technology is not going to work and could be disastrous. For example, while there were positive changes in opinion and self-reflection in a short period for graduate students in this case study, it is doubtful if the same level of cooperation can be recorded with undergraduate students. Along with the issue of time is the amount of work for the instructor: There are more messages to attend to, and quick feedback is necessary, otherwise the overall outcomes of the course and satisfaction with the technology can be destroyed.

The CMC/FtF design in the course offers the added benefit of flexibility in facilitating increased participation among students while allowing an instructor to accommodate a variety of student learning styles. Finally, the challenge is not whether a student will use mediated technology, but rather when and in what capacity? Therefore, it appears that instructors have the potential to prepare and shape how CMC is used or applied at a later time.

Bibliography

Anderson, R. S. (1998). Why talk about different ways to grade? The shift from traditional assessment to alternative assessment. In R. S. Anderson & B. W. Speck, *New directions for teaching and learning: No. 74. Changing the way we grade student performance: Classroom assessment and the new learning paradigm* (pp. 5–15). San Francisco, CA: Jossey-Bass.

Angelo, T. A. (1995, November). Reassessing (and defining) assessment. *AAHE Bulletin, 48*(3), 7.

Angelo, T. A., & Cross, K. P. (1993). *Classroom assessment techniques: A handbook for college teachers.* San Francisco, CA: Jossey-Bass.

Aronson, E. (1978). *The jigsaw classroom.* Beverly Hills, CA: Sage.

Bailey, Y. S., & Wright, V. H. (2000). *Innovative uses of threaded discussion groups* (Report No. HE033571). Bowling Green, KY: Mid South Educational Research Association. (ERIC Document Reproduction Service No. ED446716)

Bates, T. (2002, April 17). *The impact of e-learning on the university campus: Measuring the costs and benefits.* Guest lecture presented at the Knowledge Media Design Institute, University of Toronto, Canada.

Battersby, M. (1999, Fall). Guest editorial: Assessment and learning. *Learning Quarterly: Assessment and Learning, 3*(3), 2–5.

Belfer, K., & Nesbit, J. C. (2001). *GUIDE: An instrument for evaluating quality of instructional design in mixed-mode university courses.* Paper presented at the ED-MEDIA 2001 World Conference on Educational Multimedia, Hypermedia & Telecommunications, Tampere, Finland.

Belfer, K., & Wakkary, R. (2002). *Cooperative learning: Assessment of teamwork.* Paper presented at the ED-MEDIA 2002 World Conference on Educational Multimedia, Hypermedia & Telecommunications, Denver, CO. Retrieved May 20, 2004, from www2.cstudies.ubc.ca/~belfer/Papers/TeamAssess.doc

Bell, P. (2002). Science is argument: Toward sociocognitive supports for disciplinary argumentation. In T. Koschmann, R. Hall, & N. Miyake (Eds.), *CSCL 2: Carrying forward the conversation* (pp. 499–505). Mahwah, NJ: Lawrence Erlbaum.

Bereiter, C. (2002). Education in a knowledge society. In B. Smith (Ed.), *Liberal education in a knowledge society* (pp. 11–34). Peru, IL: Open Court.

Bielaczyc, K., & Collins, A. (1999). Learning communities in classrooms: A reconceptualization of educational practice. In C. M. Reigeluth (Ed.), *Instructional-design theories and models: A new paradigm of instructional theory* (pp. 269–292). Mahwah, NJ: Lawrence Erlbaum.

Biggs, J. B. (1996). Enhancing teaching through constructive alignment. *Higher Education, 32*(3), 347–364.

Bloom, B. S. (Ed.). (1956). *Taxonomy of educational objectives: The classification of educational goals: Handbook I, cognitive domain.* New York, NY: Longmans, Green.

Botturi, L. (2003). *E²ML: Educational environment modeling language.* Paper presented at the ED-MEDIA 2003 World Conference on Educational Multimedia, Hypermedia & Telecommunications, Honolulu, HI. Retrieved May 20, 2004, from http://www.istituti.usilu.net/botturil/web/publications/e2ml_paper_edmedia03.pdf

Boud, D. (1995a). Assessment and learning: Contradictory or complementary? In P. Knight (Ed.), *Assessment for learning in higher education* (pp. 35–48). London, England: Kogan Page.

Boud, D. (1995b). *Enhancing learning through self assessment.* London, England: Kogan Page.

Brandon, D. P., & Hollingshead, A. B. (1999). Collaborative learning and computer-supported groups. *Communication Education, 48*(2), 109–126.

Brown, A. L., & Campione, J. C. (1994). Guided discovery in a community of learners. In K. McGilly (Ed.), *Classroom lessons: Integrating cognitive theory and classroom practice* (pp. 229–270). Cambridge, MA: MIT Press.

Brufee, K. A. (1993). *Collaborative learning: Higher education, interdependence, and the authority of knowledge.* Baltimore, MD: Johns Hopkins University Press.

Canales, J. (2003). *Enhancing online education at El Paso Community College.* Paper presented at the Community College Leadership Program, Austin, TX.

Chickering, A. W., & Gamson, Z. F. (1987, March). Seven principles for good practice in undergraduate education. *AAHE Bulletin, 39*(7), 3–7.

Cho, W., Schmelzer, C. D., & McMahon, P. S. (2002). Preparing hospitality managers for the 21st century: The merging of just-in-time education, critical thinking, and collaborative learning. *Journal of Hospitality & Tourism Research, 26*(1), 23–37.

Clark, M. (1993). Transformation learning. In S. Meriam (Ed.), *New directions for adult and continuing education: No. 57. An update on adult learning theory* (pp. 25–35). San Francisco, CA: Jossey-Bass.

Coate, J. (1997). Cyberspace innkeeping: Building online community. In P. E. Agre & D. Schuler (Eds.), *Reinventing technology, rediscovering community: Critical explorations of computing as social practice* (pp. 165–189). Greenwich: Ablex.

Cole, R. S., Slocum, L. E., & Towns, M. H. (2003). *Computer supported collaborative learning in physical chemistry: Assessment of a piloted PCOL module.* Manuscript in preparation.

Collison, G., Elbaum, B., Haavind, S., & Tinker, R. (2002). *Facilitating online learning: Effective strategies for moderators.* Madison, WI: Atwood.

Comeaux, P. (Ed.). (2002). *Communication and collaboration in the online classroom: Examples and applications.* Bolton, MA: Anker.

Comeaux, P., & McKenna-Byington, E. (2003). Computer-mediated communication in online and conventional classrooms: Some implications for instructional design and professional development programmes. *Innovations in Education and Teaching International, 40*(4), 348–355.

Comeaux, P., & Nixon, M. A. (2000). Collaborative learning in an Internet graduate course: A case study analysis. *WebNet Journal: Internet Technologies, Applications & Issues, 2*(4), 34–43.

Courtney, K., & Patalong, S. (2002, January). Integrated information skills: A case study using the Virtual Learning Environment WebCT. *Education Libraries Journal, 45*(1), 7–11.

Covey, S. R. (1989). *The 7 habits of highly effective people.* New York: Simon and Schuster.

Crafton, L. K. (1983). Learning from reading: What happens when students generate their own background information? *Journal of Reading, 26,* 586–592.

Cross, K. P. (1998). *What do we know about students' learning and how do we know it?* Paper presented at the American Association for Higher Education National Conference on Higher Education, Atlanta, GA. Retrieved March 31, 2004, from http://www.aahe.org/nche/cross_lecture.htm

Cuban, L. (2001). New technologies in old universities. In *Oversold and underused: Computers in the classroom* (pp. 99–130). Cambridge, MA: Harvard University Press.

Curtis, D., & Lawson, M. (2001). Exploring collaborative online learning. *Journal of Asynchronous Learning Networks, 5*(1), 21–34.

Daniels, H. (1994). *Literature circles: Voice and choice in the student-centered classroom.* York, ME: Stenhouse.

Davidson, A., & Orsini-Jones, M. (2002). Motivational factors in students' online learning. In S. Fallows & R. Bhanot (Eds.), *Educational development through information and communications technologies* (pp. 73–85). London, England: Kogan Page.

Department for Education and Skills. (2003). *The future of higher education.* Retrieved May 26, 2004, fromhttp://www.dfes.gov.uk/hegateway/strategy/hestrategy/expand.shtml

Drucker, P. (1985). *Innovation and entrepreneurship: Practice and principles.* New York, NY: Harper and Row.

Eanet, M. G., & Manzo, A. V. (1976). REAP—A strategy for improving reading/writing/study skills. *Journal of Reading, 19,* 647–652.

Feenberg, A. (1989). A user's guide to the pragmatics of computer-mediated communication. *Semiotica, 75,* 257–278.

Fenwick, T., & Parsons, J. (2000). *The art of evaluation: A handbook for educators and trainers.* Toronto, Ontario: Thompson Educational.

Gallini, J. (2001, March/April). A framework for the design of research in technology-mediated learning environments: A sociocultural perspective. *Educational Technology, 41*(2), 15–21.

Gunawardena, L., Lowe, C., & Anderson, T. (1997). Interaction analysis of a global online debate and the development of a constructivist interaction analysis model for computer conferencing. *Journal of Educational Computing Research, 17*(4), 395–429.

Hall, T., & Wright, T. (2002). *Guess who's coming to lunch?* Paper presented at the Computer Supported Collaborative Learning Conference, Boulder, CO. Retrieved May 24, 2004, from http://richie.idc.ul.ie/tony/guess_who_is_coming.html

Harp, W. (1991). Principles of assessment and evaluation in whole language classrooms. In W. Harp (Ed.), *Assessment and evaluation in whole language programs* (pp. 35–50). Norwood, MA: Christopher Gordon.

Hazari, S., & Schno, D. (1999). Leveraging student feedback to improve teaching in web-based courses. *T.H.E. Journal, 26*(11), 30–32.

Hofmann, J. (2001, April). Blended learning case study. *Learning Circuits.* Retrieved April 30, 2003, from http://www.learningcircuits.org/2001/apr2001/hofmann.html

Hofmeister, D., & Thomas, M. M. (2001). Virtual literature circles: Message board discussions for strengthening literacy. *Proceedings of the Society for Information Technology Teacher Education*, 2216–2219.

Honebein, P., Duffy, T. M., & Fishman, B. (1993). Constructivism and design of learning environments: Context and authentic activities for learning. In T. M. Duffy, J. Lowyck, & D. Jonassen (Eds.), *The design of constructivist learning environments: Implications for instructional design and the use of technology* (pp. 87–108). Heidelberg, Germany: Springer-Verlag.

Huba, M. E., & Freed, J. E. (2000). *Learner-centered assessment on college campuses: Shifting the focus from teaching to learning.* Boston, MA: Allyn and Bacon.

Iowa Central Community College. (2002). *Request for a change in educational offerings, 2002* (NCA report). Fort Dodge, IA: Author.

Isaacs, G. (2002). *Assessing group tasks.* Queensland, Australia: The University of Queensland, Teaching & Educational Development Institute. Retrieved January 8, 2004, from http://www.tedi.uq.edu.au/downloads/T&L_Assess_group_tasks.pdf

Johnson, D. W., Johnson, R. T., & Holubec, E. J. (1993). *Cooperation in the classroom* (Rev. ed.). Edina, MN: Interaction Book.

Joia, L. A. (2002). Analyzing a web-based e-commerce learning community: A case study in Brazil. *Internet Research: Electronic Networking Applications and Policy, 12*(4), 305–317.

Koschmann, T. (2002). Dewey's contribution to the foundations of CSCL research. In G. Stahl (Ed.), *Computer support for collaborative learning: Foundations for a CSCL community* (CSCL 2002 proceedings; pp. 17–22). Mahwah, NJ: Lawrence Erlbaum.

Krueger, R. A. (1994). *Focus groups: A practical guide for applied research* (2nd ed.). Thousand Oaks, CA: Sage.

Laurillard, D. (1993). *Rethinking university education: A framework for the effective use of educational technology.* London, England: Routledge.

Laurillard, D. (2003, October 23). *E-learning: Towards a unified strategy.* Paper presented at the ESRC Seminar Series, Educational Research and the Design of Interactive Media, Westminster, London.

Lawless, C., Smee, P., & O'Shea, T. (1998). Using concept sorting and concept mapping in business and public administration, and in education: An overview. *Educational Research, 40*(2), 219–235.

Lea, M., & Spears, R. (1992). Paralanguage and social perception in computer-mediated communication. *Journal of Organizational Computing, 2,* 321–341.

Levin, J., Kim, H., & Riel, M. (1990). Analysing instructional interactions on electronic message networks. In L. Harasim (Ed.), *Online education: Perspectives on a new environment* (pp. 185–214). New York, NY: Praeger.

Maki, P. (2001). *Program review assessment.* Paper presented to the Committee on Undergraduate Academic Program Review, Raleigh, NC.

Manzo, A. V., Manzo, U. C., & Albee, J. A. (2002). iREAP: Improving reading, writing, and thinking in the wired classroom. *Journal of Adolescent & Adult Literacy, 46*(1), 42–47.

Manzo, A. V., Manzo, U. C., & Estes, T. H. (2001). *Content area literacy: Fusing curriculum, culture, & community in the wired world* (3rd ed.). New York, NY: John Wiley & Sons.

Martin, D. C., Lorton, M., Blanc, R. A., & Evans, C. (1977). *The learning center: A comprehensive model for colleges and universities.* Kansas City, MO: University of Missouri.

Mason, R. (1992). Evaluation methodologies for computer conferencing applications. In A. Kaye (Ed.), *Collaborative learning through computer conferencing: The Najaden papers* (pp. 54–69). Berlin, Germany: Springer-Verlag.

Mathieson, K., & Keil, M. (1998, November 2). Beyond the interface: Ease of use and task/technology fit. *Information & Management, 34*(4), 221–230.

Mcdonald, J. (2003). Assessing online collaborative learning: Process and product. *Computers & Education, 40*(4), 377–391.

McGovern, G. (2002, March 18). The myth of interactivity on the Internet. *New Thinking.* Retrieved April 25, 2002, from http://www.gerrymcgovern.com/nt/2002/nt_2002_03_18_interactivity.htm

McKernan, J. (1992). *Curriculum action research.* London, England: Kogan Page.

McLoughlin, C. (2002). Computer supported teamwork: An integrative approach to evaluating cooperative online learning. *Australian Journal of Educational Technology, 18*(2), 227–254.

Merrill, D. M. (2002, August). A pebble-in-the-pond model of instructional development. *Performance Improvement, 41*(7), 39–44. Retrieved May 24, 2004, from http://www.ispi.org/pdf/Merrill.pdf

Mioduser, D., Nachmias, R., Lahav, O., & Oren, A. (2000). Web-based learning environments: Current pedagogical and technological state. *Journal of Research on Computing in Education, 33*(1), 55–76.

Moore, M. G. (2002). What does research say about the learners using computer-mediated communication in distance learning? *The American Journal of Distance Education, 16*(2), 61–64. Retrieved May 25, 2004, from http://www.ajde.com/Documents/AJDE1602_1.pdf

Morgan, C., & O'Reilly, M. (2001). Innovations in online assessment. In F. Lockwood & A. Gooley (Eds.), *Innovations in open & distance learning: Successful development of online and web-based learning* (pp. 179–188). London, England: Kogan Page.

Morrison, D. (2003, Fall). Using activity theory to design constructivist online learning environments for higher order thinking: A retrospective analysis. *Canadian Journal of Learning and Technology, 29*(3), 21–35.

Mowrer, D. E. (1996). A content analysis of student/instructor communication via computer conferencing. *Higher Education, 32,* 217–241.

Muhr, T. (1997). *ATLAS.ti: The knowledge workbench.* Berlin, Germany: Scientific Software Development.

Nelson, G. E. (1998, April). *On-line evaluation: Multiple choice, discussion questions, essay, and authentic projects.* Paper presented at the third Teaching in the Community Colleges Online Conference, Honolulu, HI.

Ng, K. C. (2001). Using e-mail to foster collaboration in distance education. *Open Learning, 16*(2), 191–200.

Noble, D. (1999) *Digital diploma mill, part IV: Rehearsal for the revolution.* Retrieved May 24, 2004, from http://www.communication. ucsd.edu/dl/ddm4.html

Noble, D. (2002, February 20). *The rise and demise of on-line education.* Guest lecture presented at the Knowledge Media Design Institute, University of Toronto, Canada.

Norman, D. A. (1993). *Things that make us smart: Defending human attributes in the age of the machine.* Reading, MA: Addison-Wesley.

O'Banion, T. (1997). *A learning college for the 21st century.* Phoenix, AZ: Oryx Press.

Olaniran, B. A. (1994). Group performance in computer-mediated communication and face to face meetings. *Management Communication Quarterly, 7,* 256–281.

Olaniran, B. A. (1995). Perceived communication outcomes in computer-mediated communication: An analysis of three systems among new users. *Information Processing and Management, 31,* 525–541.

Oliver, R. (2000). When teaching meets learning: Design principles and strategies for web-based learning environments that support knowledge construction. *ASCILITE* 2000 conference proceedings. Retrieved March 17, 2004, from http://www.ascilite.org.au/confer ences/coffs00/papers/ron_oliver_keynote.pdf

Orsini-Jones, M. (2003, July). *Student-centered evaluation of WebCT in a "blended delivery" course.* Paper presented at the fifth annual WebCT User Conference, San Diego, CA.

Orsini-Jones, M., & Davidson, A. (1999, May/June). From reflective learners to reflective lecturers via WebCT. *Active Learning, 10,* 32–38.

Palmer, P. J. (1998). *The courage to teach: Exploring the inner landscape of a teacher's life.* San Francisco, CA: Jossey-Bass.

Papert, S. (1996). A word for learning. In Y. Kasai & M. Resnick (Eds.), *Constructionism in practice: Designing, thinking and learning in a digital world* (pp. 9–24). Mahwah, NJ: Lawrence Erlbaum.

Patalong, S. (2002, September). Using WebCT to support information skills teaching. *ASSIG Nation, 19*(4), 24–27.

Pittman, A., Gosper, M., & Rich, D. (1999). Internet based teaching in geography at Macquarie University. *Australian Journal of Educational technology, 15*(2), 167–187.

Race, P., & Brown, S. (2001). *The ILTA guide: Inspiring learning about teaching and assessment.* York, England: The Institute for Learning and Teaching in Higher Education and Education Guardian.

Reeves, T. C., & Okey, J. R. (1996). Alternative assessment for constructivist learning environments. In B. G. Wilson (Ed.), *Constructivist learning environments: Case studies in instructional design* (pp. 191–201). Englewood Cliffs, NJ: Educational Technology Publications.

Resnick, M. (2002). Revolutionizing learning in the digital age. In M. Devlin, R. Larson, & J. Meyerson (Eds.), *The internet and the university: 2001 forum* (pp. 45–64): Boulder, CO: EDUCAUSE.

Richards, I. A. (1951). *Practical criticism: A study of literary judgment.* New York, NY: Harcourt Brace.

Romer, R., & Education Commission of the States. (1996, April). What research says about improving undergraduate education. *AAHE Bulletin, 48*(8), 5–8.

Romiszowski, A. J. (1997). Web-based distance learning and teaching: Revolutionary invention or reaction to necessity? In B. Kahn (Ed.), *Web-based instruction* (pp. 25–37). Englewood Cliffs, NJ: Educational Technology Publications.

Rosenblatt, L. M. (1983). *Literature as exploration.* New York, NY: Modern Language Association.

Roueche, J. E., Johnson, L. F., Roueche, S. D., & Associates. (1997). *Embracing the tiger: The effectiveness debate & the community college.* Washington, DC: Community College Press.

Rovia, A. P. (2001). Building classroom community at a distance: A case study. *Educational Technology Research and Development, 49*(4), 33–48.

Salmon, G. (2002). *E-tivities: The key to active online learning.* London, England: Kogan Page.

Sanders, L. R. (2001). Improving assessment in university classrooms. *College Teaching, 49*(2), 62–64.

Scardamalia, M., & Bereiter, C. (2002). Knowledge building. In L. C. Deighton (Ed.), *Encyclopedia of education* (2nd ed.; pp. 1370–1373). New York, NY: Macmillan Reference.

Schreyer Institute for Innovative Learning. (2001). *How to develop a rubric.* University Park, PA: Author. Retrieved October 12, 2003, from http://www.inov8.psu.edu/toolbox/assessmenttools.asp

Schwartz, D. L., Bransford, J. D. (1998). A time for telling. *Cognition and Instruction, 16*(4), 475–522.

Shedletsky, L. J., & Aitkin, J. E. (2001, July). The paradoxes of online academic work. *Communication Education, 50*(3), 206–217.

Sigala, M. (2002a). The evolution of Internet pedagogy: Benefits for tourism and hospitality education. *Journal of Hospitality, Leisure, Sport & Tourism Education, 1*(2), 29–45.

Sigala, M. (2002b). *Evaluating the effectiveness of e-learning platforms in tourism and hospitality education.* Paper presented at the annual I-CHRIE Convention, Orlando, FL.

Sigala, M., & Christou, E. (2003). Enhancing and complementing the instruction of tourism and hospitality courses through the use of online educational tools. *Journal of Hospitality & Tourism Education, 15*(1), 6–16.

Slavin, R. E. (1995). *Cooperative learning: Theory, research, and practice* (2nd ed.). Boston, MA: Allyn and Bacon.

Slocum, L. E., Towns, M. H., & Zielinski, T. J. (in press). On-line chemistry modules: Interaction and effective faculty facilitation. *Journal of Chemical Education.*

Speck, B. W. (2002). Learning-teaching-assessment paradigms and the on-line classroom. In R. S. Anderson, J. F. Bauer, & B. W. Speck (Eds.), *New directions for teaching and learning: No. 91. Assessment strategies for the on-line class: From theory to practice* (pp. 5–18). San Francisco, CA: Jossey-Bass.

Stevens, R. (2002). Keeping it complex in an era of big education. In T. Koschmann, R. Hall, & N. Miyake (Eds.), *CSCL 2: Carrying forward the conversation* (pp. 269–273). Mahwah, NJ: Lawrence Erlbaum.

Taylor, S. S. (2002, May 13). Education online: Off course or on track? *Community College Week, 14,* 10–13.

Thomas, M. M. (2001). Proficient reader characteristics: Relationships among text-dependent and higher-order literacy variables with reference to stage theories of intellectual development. *Dissertation Abstracts International* (UMI No. 3010626).

Thomas, M. M., & Hofmeister, D. (2002a). Assessing the effectiveness of technology integration: Message boards for strengthening literacy. *Computers & Education, 38,* 233–240.

Thomas, M. M., & Hofmeister, D. (2002b). *Virtual learning circles: Utilizing online message board interactions for strengthening literacy development.* Paper presented at the 19th World Congress on Reading, Edinburgh, Scotland (Report No. CS511475). (ERIC Document Reproduction Service No. ED468900)

Thomas, M. M., & Hofmeister, D. (2003). Moving content area literacy into the digital age: Using online discussion board interactions. *Journal of Content Area Reading, 2*(1), 61–80.

Travis, J. E. (1996). Meaningful assessment. *Clearing House, 69*(5), 308–312.

Twigg, C. A. (2002, May). Innovations in online learning: The new pacesetters. *Learning Abstracts, 5*(5). Retrieved December 1, 2003, from http://www.league.org/publication/abstracts/learning/lelabs0205.html

Valiathan, P. (2002, August). Blended learning models. *Learning Circuits.* Retrieved May 24, 2004, from http://www.learningcircuits.org/ 2002/aug2002/valiathan.html

Wade, W. (1999, October). What do students know and how do we know they know it? *T.H.E Journal, 27,* 94–98.

Wakkary, R., & Belfer, K. (2002, October). *An evaluation framework for the development process of an online curriculum.* Paper presented at the E-Learn 2002 World Conference on E-Learning in Corporate, Government, Healthcare, & Higher Education, Montreal, Canada.

Walther, J. B. (2002). Time effects in computer-mediated groups: Past, present, and future. In P. Hinds & S. Kiesler (Eds.), *Distributed work* (pp. 235–257). Cambridge, MA: MIT Press.

Warschauer, M., & Kern, R. (2000). *Networked-based language teaching: Concepts and practice.* Cambridge, England: Cambridge University Press.

Weinstein, C. E., Corliss, S. B., Beth, A. D., Cho, Y., & Bera, S. J. (2002, November 1). Learner control: The upside and the downside of online learning. *Innovations Abstracts, 24*(25), 1–2. Retrieved May 19, 2004, from http://web.grcc.edu/CTL/innovation_abstracts/IA_XXIV_25.pdf

Wild, M., & Omari, A. (1996, July). *Developing educational content for the web: Issues and ideas.* Paper presented at AusWeb96: The second Australian World Wide Web Conference, Queensland, Australia. Retrieved March 17, 2004, from http://elmo.scu.edu.au/sponsored/ ausweb/ausweb96/educn/wild/paper.html

Williams, G., & McKercher, B. (2001). Tourism education and the Internet: Benefits, challenges and opportunities. *Journal of Teaching in Travel and Tourism, 1*(2/3), 1–15.

Yamada, C. (2002). *Applying the interactive narrative genre.* Paper presented at the E-Learn 2002 World Conference on E-Learning in Corporate, Government, Healthcare, & Higher Education, Montreal, Canada.

Yancey, K. B. (1998). Reflection, self-assessment, and learning. *Clearing House, 72*(1), 13–17.

Yu, F. (2002). The efficacy of electronic telecommunications in fostering interpersonal relationships. *Journal of Educational Computing Research, 26*(2), 213–225.

Index

A
About-Point, 75
Accountability issues, 5–6
Aitken, J. E., 112
American Association for Higher
    Education, 6
Anderson, R. S., xx
Anderson, T., 89
Angelo, T. A., xx, 5
Aronson, E., 67
Assessment
    benefits of online, xxiii, 22–23, 33
    characteristics (guidelines),
        11–12, 35–36, 37–38
    definition, 4–5
    formative, 21, 31, 97, 113–114,
        121–122, 123, 132–133
    improving instructional design,
        xxvi
    instruments, xxiv, xxv
    learning, and, xx, xxii, 38
    models for online, 19, 23–25
    peer, 37, 47
    performance-based, 22–23
    pre-, 9
    qualitative methods, 90–91
    quantitative evaluation, 44–45,
        46, 90
    self-, 28–29, 31, 37, 45
    summative, 25, 113–114,
        19–120, 123, 132–133

team, 32
traditional methods, 13–14
Authentic (real-world) projects, xxii,
    xxiii, xxiv, 21, 22, 23, 26–27,
    57, 60, 105, 107

B
Bailey, Y. S., 73
Bates, T., 99
Battersby, M., 37
Belfer, K., 34, 41, 54
Bell, P., 105, 107
Bera, S. J., 16
Bereiter, C., 56, 70
Bielaczye, K., 56
Biggs, J. B., 19
Blackboard, 75
Blanc, R. A., 75
Blended learning, 100, 106, 128,
    131, 144, 149–150
Bloom, B. S., 17
Boeing Leadership Center, 106
Boud, D., xx, xxi, 38, 133
Brandon D. P., 112
Bransford, J. D., 25
Brown, A. L., 56, 67
Brown, L., 110
Brown, S., 133
Bruffee, K. A., 112
Business education, 56–57